THE
EVERYTHING®
GUIDE TO
NETWORK MARKETING

Dear Reader,

Network marketing, multilevel marketing (MLM), direct sales, relationship marketing—while there are different names for this industry, one thing is constant: It offers the average person a chance to see her dreams come true, if she is willing to learn and dedicate the necessary time and energy.

My network marketing career began in my early twenties, as I walked long blocks, dropping off brochures, hoping to sell cologne and make a few dollars. Over the next few years I tried selling a variety of other things—soap, powdered milk, air purifiers, and even worms—but I still didn't really understand what network marketing was. Later I worked in commission sales for twelve years. All of these opportunities added to my education and eventual success in network marketing.

Today, after nine years in an MLM company and earnings of over $5 million, my desire is to help other people learn and succeed earlier than I did in networking marketing. Each chapter in this book will add to your education, and give you information you'll need to find the right company for you. Then, as you build your business, you'll meet new and interesting people, travel to different cities and countries, and find countless people within your company who *want* you to succeed!

Let's get started!

Esther Spina

Welcome to the EVERYTHING Series!

These handy, accessible books give you all you need to tackle a difficult project, gain a new hobby, or even brush up on something you learned back in school but have since forgotten. You can choose to read from cover to cover or just pick out information from our four useful boxes.

 Alerts

Urgent warnings

 Facts

Important snippets of information

 **Essentials**

Quick handy tips

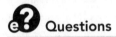 **Questions**

Answers to common questions

When you're done reading, you can finally say you know **EVERYTHING®**!

PUBLISHER Karen Cooper

MANAGING EDITOR, EVERYTHING® SERIES Lisa Laing

COPY CHIEF Casey Ebert

ACQUISITIONS EDITOR Lisa Laing

DEVELOPMENT EDITOR Brett Palana-Shanahan

EVERYTHING® SERIES COVER DESIGNER Erin Alexander

Visit the entire Everything® series at *www.everything.com*

THE
EVERYTHING®
GUIDE TO
NETWORK
MARKETING

A step-by-step plan for multilevel
marketing success

Esther Spina

adamsmedia
Avon, Massachusetts

To my son David, who at twenty-five years old introduced me to the real business of network marketing and the success that is possible. Also to my other two sons, Aaron and Peter, who followed me in the journey.

An Everything® Series Book.
Everything® and everything.com® are registered trademarks of F+W Media, Inc.

Published by
Adams Media, a division of F+W Media, Inc.
57 Littlefield Street, Avon, MA 02322. U.S.A.
www.adamsmedia.com

Contains material adapted from *The Everything® Network Marketing Book* by Margaret Kaeter, copyright © 2003 by F+W Media, Inc., ISBN 10: 1-58062-736-6, ISBN 13: 978-1-58062-736-8.

ISBN 10: 1-4405-9234-9
ISBN 13: 978-1-4405-9234-8
eISBN 10: 1-4405-9235-7
eISBN 13: 978-1-4405-9235-5

Printed in the United States of America.

10 9 8 7 6 5 4 3 2 1

Library of Congress Cataloging-in-Publication Data
Spina, Esther.
  The everything guide to network marketing / Esther Spina.
      pages cm
  Includes index.
  ISBN 978-1-4405-9234-8 (pb) -- ISBN 1-4405-9234-9 (pb) -- ISBN 978-1-4405-9235-5 (ebook) -- ISBN 1-4405-9235-7 (ebook)
  1. Multilevel marketing. I. Title.
  HF5415.126.S67 2015
  658.8'72--dc23

                          2015026611

This book is available at quantity discounts for bulk purchases.
For information, please call 1-800-289-0963.

Contents

Acknowledgments

My success would not be possible without the co-founders of Ambit Energy and their vision to create not only a billion-dollar energy empire but an opportunity for financial freedom to countless numbers of people, including myself and my family.

Jere Thompson Jr., the CEO, for the integrity he displays on a daily basis in every decision that inspires you to do the same ("Never sacrifice integrity for growth.").

Chris Chambless, CMO, the mastermind of the comp plan that pays everyone and keeps them happy (and the first person who showed me the plan and how to be successful in this business).

John Burke, CIO, the best CIO in the world and the genius behind Ambit, creating the massive back-office machine and multimillion-dollar system that keeps everything running smoothly.

Ken Dunn, one of the greatest network marketers and prospectors of people I have met. His encouragement and belief inspires me to keep going and stay the course.

Simon Presland and Faouzi Daghistani, who transformed my knowledge, ideas, and thoughts and turned them into reality and a guide for *The Everything® Guide to Network Marketing*.

To all the people I have had relationships in my network marketing journey, some good and some not so good. You have helped to teach me many things about business, life, and myself.

Lastly, but not least, I thank God for helping me to persevere and enjoy this great business, my husband for his support, and my children and grandchildren, who are my why and passion and to whom I leave this wonderful opportunity and legacy.

The Top 10 Benefits
of Network Marketing

1. The initial investment, compared to most businesses, is relatively low. This categorizes it as an almost "risk-free" opportunity.
2. Building your business offers you the opportunity to meet many new people who will often share your passion for entrepreneurship and promoting a particular line of products or services.
3. As your business grows, you will be offered exciting travel opportunities to help support your team or attend training functions in exotic locations.
4. You succeed in this business by helping others win, too; a major point of difference when it comes to the way other industries may operate.
5. You earn the income you're willing to work toward. There are no barriers to your commissions, as long as you are prepared to work toward creating the sales volume required.
6. As you develop a bigger income, you can choose to build the business solely and forego other employment requirements.
7. Companies and team leaders go out of their way to recognize top achievers. If you've always felt your efforts were not recognized, network marketing will provide you with ample opportunities to be in the spotlight.
8. The personal and leadership development offered is second to none, allowing you to strengthen your people and communication skills.
9. You'll have the chance to inspire others to get out of their comfort zones and reach for their own personal dreams and goals.
10. The industry is on a rising curve, growing yearly. The sooner you get involved and get active, the stronger possibility you have of taking advantage of a thriving business trend.

Introduction

The network marketing/direct selling profession has grown dramatically in the 100-plus years of its existence. What originally began as ideas to help motivate and reward independent sellers—with Avon in 1886, the Fuller Brush Company in 1906, and the vitamin supplements produced by Nutrilite and first sold door-to-door in 1945—has now developed into an industry that, as of 2013, brought in yearly sales exceeding $178 billion. To give you a perspective of how significant that is on a global scale, compare that figure to other major industries that operate on a worldwide level. In that same year the music industry grossed $15 billion, the Hollywood movie business did $88 billion, and the video game industry earned $76 billion.

The Direct Selling Association reports that network marketing is now conducted in more than 100 countries around the world, with more than 56 million people participating. The industry continues to develop and has attracted the attention and praise of the business community and the financial press. It could be argued that it is the only real option left in the free enterprise system where people can build financial freedom without a large investment of their time or money.

Economic uncertainty, a downturn in the job market, and a public wary of Wall Street has seen many look to this business as a way to create financial security and protect their income. It is also one of the best ways to create passive residual income, with the option of working it part-time. True financial freedom is not how much money you make, but that you have enough money coming in every month that you don't have to work for. That's what network marketing can do for you.

While at first it may appear to be a male-dominated industry, there are many women who have found their own personal success sharing things they love, and making money at it as well. For example, there are clothes, jewelry, linens, even beauty and aging products that are being shared through network marketing.

Every person who joins a network marketing company has his or her own unique reasons, and surprisingly it is not always for the money. Many times it is for the social aspect of the business, as you will add hundreds and even thousands of new people to your social circle through this amazing industry. As you read through this guide, those special reasons will come to you. You'll determine if this industry is right for you and why. You'll understand a little of its history, and what there is to look forward to if you choose to get involved. Whether you are new to the profession or have developed a million-dollar income, *The Everything® Guide to Network Marketing* is designed to help you gain greater insights into today's trends, tools, and strategies.

Network marketing isn't for everybody. It may not be for you. But it could end up being the most exciting, most rewarding career choice you ever make. And besides that, it is a really fun business!

You will only ever know by getting started.

The journey begins here.

CHAPTER 1

A Business for Today's Economy

A s the economy evolves, businesses are searching for alternatives to bring their products and services to consumers. But at the same time, marketing and distribution can be a major drain on a company's bottom line. Business owners are constantly searching for new marketing and distribution solutions, and network marketing has many of the answers. Companies such as Amazon, Verizon, Rodan + Fields, Sprint Communications, and DirecTV have added network marketing or reward-for-referral type structures to their marketing efforts, implementing an independent word-of-mouth sales force that helps create awareness of their products where conventional advertising may not have worked.

Defining Network Marketing

Marketing is the process that businesses or professions use to make consumers aware of a product or service so they can be guided into making a decision. Many people see sales and marketing as a combined function, but they have distinct differences. While marketing is an integral part of the selling process, marketers focus more on creating appeal for the product. This in turn helps create a proactive buyer who makes a purchase with or without a salesperson being present.

Network marketing is a marketing and distribution method that consists of independent team members or salespeople who are rewarded for marketing the product or service within the guidelines set by the company. These team members may have different titles with different companies; for example, some are called distributors, consultants, or representatives. This book uses all those terms interchangeably.

 Question

Why don't all companies use network marketing?
Network marketing is the right choice for products that are easy to display or explain. Items that are small and easily sold to individual people in small amounts often work well with this business model. Objects such as motor vehicles and large pieces of equipment are not as easily promoted through network marketing.

Network marketing reps not only use and sell a company's products and/or services themselves, but they also have the opportunity to invite others to become part of their network to use and share the service. When this process occurs, the company rewards reps, usually financially, based on the volume of sales produced by the newly created network. Network marketers like to use the term "relationship marketing," as most of them do not see themselves as selling but as sharing the product, service, or business.

Over the years, these types of businesses have been called many things, including network marketing, multilevel marketing (MLM), referral or relationship marketing, a people's franchise, and direct sales. The most common term used today is the one that will be used in this book, which is network marketing.

Whatever they're called, businesses in this category utilize independent representatives to reach potential customers that the company otherwise would not reach with traditional online or offline marketing methods.

While direct selling and affiliate marketing are often aligned with network marketing, both of these methods usually lack one factor: the representative's ability to grow an organization on which she earns an income from total group sales. However, several direct-sales companies such as Tupperware, Lorraine Lea, Cabi, and Avon have created incentives for their reps to not only directly sell the product to an end consumer, but also to help bring in new consultants.

 Alert

Be wary of any marketing that screams out, "This is not network marketing." Promoters often try to attract those who are wary of the industry but actually unsure of what is involved. If the business you are looking at involves you moving a product through a team of distributors, it is most likely a network marketing business.

Franchising and Network Marketing

During the Industrial Revolution, as the American economy blossomed, the European idea of granting a license to a professional in order to carry on a specific business began to take hold. Henry Ford used franchises in order to increase sales and exposure of his first Ford automobile, and Coca-Cola also entered the market in 1899. It wasn't until the 1950s, however, that the franchise model really boomed. McDonald's, Kentucky Fried Chicken (now KFC), 7-Eleven, and Dunkin' Donuts found undeniable success with the franchise business model. The International Franchise Association estimates that franchises earn a combined $1.5 trillion in revenues each year.

One of the similarities between franchising and network marketing is the turnkey factor of starting a business. Franchises appeal to business owners who prefer a ready-made system that they can plug into and get to work with right away. Network marketing is the same in many aspects. Marketing and promotional tools, major administrative decisions, and product warehousing and distribution are all handled by the company, while the franchise owner or independent network marketer is free to focus on growing and maintaining his business.

 Essential

Elizabeth Timothy, a journalist and newspaper editor, was the first woman in the United States to obtain a franchise. Her husband Lewis happened to be working for the publisher and future governor of Pennsylvania, Benjamin Franklin, and in 1733 entered into an agreement with Franklin to create a six-year franchise of the *South Carolina Gazette* newspaper. When he died five years into the contract in a freak accident, Elizabeth was granted permission to take over, growing the franchise to such an extent that Franklin highly praised her business and management skills.

Direct Selling and Network Marketing

The system of network marketing originated with the idea of rewarding direct sellers with stronger incentives to market and sell products. For hundreds of years, selling directly to one's family and friends was a conventional and expected way of doing business. In the early 1940s, Carl Rehnborg, founder of the company Nutrilite, helped create the first multilevel plan that rewarded salespeople by allowing them to contract other direct sellers and earn discounts on their product in return for increased sales. Rehnborg was passionate about his product, but was unprepared for the burdensome task of training new sales representatives in how to sell the product and explain its benefits.

In association with two of his most successful representatives, he drew up a plan that moved away from a direct-to-customer model, allowing his representatives to not only sell product but also create a team of sellers and profit from their revenue growth. In effect, this caused a split between traditional direct selling and the new model eventually known as network marketing.

Today there are many companies, such as Avon, Mary Kay, Premier Designs, and Tupperware that combine the benefits of direct-to-consumer selling with the advantages of network marketing. Newer companies for women include Jamberry Nails, Doterra Oils, and Stella & Dot. While still operating under the basic model of obtaining a product from the company and selling it through a home party or friendly get-together, these companies now encourage consultants to invite others to come on board as consultants and be rewarded with their sales as well.

 Fact

Not all companies are driven by physical products. Many companies, such as Ambit Energy and Legal Shield, offer services related to utilities and consumer protection and are available to their consultants and to retail customers. This doesn't mean that choosing a product over a service or vice versa will give you a greater chance to succeed, or that one is better than the other. At the end of the day it will come down to what you see yourself using and comfortably recommending to others.

Industry Jargon

As you progress in network marketing and begin to meet others in the industry, whether you are totally part-time or have gone full-time, there are certain terms that will start to pop up almost immediately. Here's a brief guide to some of the most common industry terms:

- **Achievement or promotion level:** The rank or title a rep has attained based on a level of sales or other benchmarks. Different companies use different terms for these levels, including Supervisor, Executive, National, Pearl, or Diamond. A company's rank advancement chart will list its titles and what it takes to achieve them.
- **Bonus pool:** An income fund that is set aside from global sales or sales during a specific period that is distributed as a reward for qualified leaders.
- **Breakage:** A portion of commissions that are unpaid to the rep and kept by the company due to unachieved sales volumes or targets not being met during the qualification period.
- **Business presentation (BP) or business opportunity presentation (BOP):** A meeting or business presentation held in a coffee shop, restaurant, home, or hotel conference room where the prime focus is on inviting others to become independent reps or product customers.
- **Buyback policy:** An agreement by a company to buy back products from reps at a preset value if they are returned within a specified period.
- **BV:** The real value a company uses to assess commissions payable. Often referred to as either business volume or bonus volume, this is rarely the same as the wholesale dollar value and will differ from company to company.
- **Coding bonus:** A bonus that some companies use to pay reps based on their downline performance. Sales made by a representative's downline reps are coded so that the original rep is paid a bonus on their initial order, over and above their ongoing sales and personal orders.

- **Cold market:** Prospects for your business who are outside your usual circle of friends, family, or associates.
- **Compression:** A type of compensation plan that compresses the downline by one level if a rep quits or is terminated. The team member that is positioned below the relinquished level is then moved up into the newly vacated position.
- **Depth:** The number of levels in a personal network.
- **Direct selling:** Selling a product, usually face-to-face, outside of a conventional retail outlet. Sales of this type are usually made at a home, hotel, or hall such as a civic center.
- **Downline:** The distributors, reps, or consultants in your own organization who came in after you are referred to as your downline. They are your downline whether you have personally brought them in or someone in your team has.
- **Drop-ship or autoship:** When products are sent directly from the company to the purchaser's door rather than being delivered by a rep. This is a common and convenient practice for most network marketing companies today.
- **Duplication:** The process of following a proven and successful system.
- **Frontline:** A rep who is personally sponsored by you and is placed first directly under you. Companies may limit how many reps you can have in your frontline, or allow you to sponsor as many as you can but place them in different parts of your organization.
- **Heavy hitter:** A leader who has created both large teams and huge sales volume on a consistent basis.
- **Home meeting:** An opportunity meeting held in a rep's home. This is very often the first presentation for new reps to family and friends.
- **Hotel meeting:** An opportunity meeting held in a rented hotel conference room.

- **Leg:** A downline organization that begins with someone you have personally sponsored that then grows down in multiple levels in depth.
- **Momentum:** A swift growth period where sales and the introduction of new customers and reps rapidly accelerates.
- **Monthly volume requirements:** The sales volume you need to produce in order to satisfy certain commission requirements.
- **Payout:** The percentages of revenue that a company pays in the form of commissions to qualified reps. Most companies today pay between 40–70 percent back to their reps as some form of compensation.
- **Prelaunch:** A period of months during which a company sets itself up and creates a major marketing push prior to its official launch.
- **Prospect:** A potential customer or recruit.
- **Prospecting:** The process of seeking product customers or new team members to help grow your organization.
- **Personal volume (PV):** The amount of product that you buy at wholesale from the company for your personal use.
- **Sponsor:** The person who introduced and signed you into the business. A sponsor is also responsible for your training, support, and guidance in the business.
- **Teleconference:** A conference held over the phone with reps dialing in from any location. Teleconferences are often used when relaying major news or creating a major push to bring in new team members and customers.
- **Three-way calls:** Used as a training method and prospecting technique, a three-way call allows a team member to bring a more experienced colleague into a conversation with a prospective team member. The experienced team member explains the business and answers questions, which helps instill confidence in both the new rep and the prospect.

- **Upline:** Your sponsor and the line of reps above your sponsor.
- **Warm list:** A list of contacts that includes your friends, family, and close acquaintances that is used to determine which ones can be approached regarding your business, product, or service.
- **Webcast or webinar:** An online presentation that reps, prospects, and customers can view live online instead of having to travel to hear the presentation. Many webcasts are also recorded, making them a valuable training tool.
- **Width:** the number of people that your company compensation plan dictates you can have on your first level. In some cases it is limited to two, and in many there are no limits.

 Essential

Your sponsor has a direct interest in your success. The sales volume you create and the new reps you bring on board make your sponsor's earnings greater every month. Because of this, you should never be hesitant in asking for her help.

The Perfect Business?

One of the biggest benefits for those looking at network marketing for the first time is the relative ease it takes to get involved. It doesn't require past experience in sales or business. It doesn't require you to have a high education level. There are no age restrictions, although most companies will require you to be at least eighteen years of age in order to get started. You will need to be able to access e-mail and your company's website to view your volume and team growth, but you won't need to be an Internet whiz to do all that. There are also no restrictions on your sex, height, race, or background.

People from any background can be successful in this business if they choose to be. It's all a matter of choice, and then being persistent and committed enough to stick with that decision in order to achieve your goals. The best part is that it literally is a "part-time" business.

So is a network marketing business the perfect business? No business will ever be perfect. But it is a great business model that encompasses the American free enterprise system and gives you the chance to achieve your financial goals and dreams.

 Fact

According to the Direct Selling Association, approximately one in four Americans will give network marketing a try at some point in their lives. Most will quit after less than one year, but about 10 percent of those who try it will make a career of it.

The low cost of entry, the ability to work your own hours, the support of other team members who are invested in your success, and the opportunity to create almost any income level combine to make this a business with advantages like no other. Add in the fact that you can operate this business anywhere in the world, as long as you have access to a phone and the Internet, and you can start to see why so many people see network marketing as the business of the future.

A New Generation of Network Marketers

What was once viewed as a business for those who were struggling to earn a dime or for housewives wanting to help balance the family budget is now a multibillion-dollar industry attracting people from all walks of life. As the financial press and entrepreneurial icons such as Warren Buffett and Donald Trump (both own a network marketing company) tout the benefits of network marketing, a new generation has awakened to what may be the business world's best-kept secret.

Parents who are choosing to work from home, retirees, and those who are worn out with the corporate world are looking to this industry and its generous benefits. Moms who are eager to spend more time at home with their children have used their network marketing income to help stay financially independent while engaging in more quality time with their family instead of devoting hours to an employer. That's exactly what Mary Crowley did as a single mom during the Great Depression. From her simple beginning, she honed her business skills and created a multimillion-dollar business to help women decorate beautiful homes at a reasonable price with her company Home Interiors & Gifts.

For many years, the baby-boomer generation provided the industry with a fertile ground for new recruits. These men and women were excited by the lure of greater wealth and products that promised to help restore their youth, vitality, and appearance. Companies such as Mary Kay, Herbalife, Amway, and Shaklee proved highly appealing to a public open to new ideas and financial opportunities. Women in particular were intrigued by the chance to have their own home-based business—one in which their natural talents of networking, sharing, and nurturing others were rewarded with new cars, luxury trips, and an income that a CEO would envy.

Younger millennials are fueling a resurgence in network marketing's appeal and growth. Many aren't ready for a typical corporate career but delight in the chance to create their own lifestyle, unencumbered by the routine of an office environment or having to play by rules effectively created in their grandparents' era. They want to travel more, do more, and have more, and they enjoy the pursuit of finding ways to do all that earlier in their lives. Network marketing provides millennials with that opportunity, and they are increasingly choosing to run with it.

CHAPTER 2

The Rise of Network Marketing

N etwork marketing has not only helped change the lives of those that choose to build a part-time business, but it has helped bring a multitude of unique products into the hands of consumers. The rise of network marketing has created a new generation of entrepreneurs, initially dominated by those from the baby-boomer generation in search of ways to fulfill both material and personal desires. Network marketing is a proven, highly successful way of developing an income. It's one of the few business methods that allows you to operate in a way that suits your personal lifestyle while also providing the support and structure of a larger organization.

The Birth of an Industry

Direct selling was the norm more than 2,000 years ago, when merchants traveled by caravan throughout Greece, Rome, India, and much of the Middle East, offering their goods to neighboring tribes and villages. The direct-sales occupation was a necessary part of the economy and allowed commerce to flourish in areas where many food items, wines, and household goods were in constant need.

Selling directly to the consumer continued to flourish throughout the world as transportation evolved, allowing hawkers and merchants to travel to new communities in areas they previously considered unreachable.

 Fact

Seventy-four percent of adults in the Unites States have purchased products from someone they know who is involved in direct selling.

One of these opportunities was the newly discovered America, where Europeans in the 1600s were steadily migrating to and establishing fresh foundations. Gypsies in particular, skilled in the art of selling, continued to ply their trade in a land rapidly filling with a population in need of their wares.

In 1886, a book salesman from New York discovered that the little bottles of perfume he was adding as a gift with every order on his door-to-door route were becoming more popular than the books he was selling. It didn't take David H. McConnell long to realize that if these perfumes were in such high demand, perhaps it was a better idea to focus on them as his major line of business. McConnell went on to establish the California Perfume Company, the company now known as Avon Products.

Avon changed the commercial landscape by practically creating a business exclusively for women, and in particular, housewives. Women now had the opportunity to create their own financial independence, an idea that was almost unheard of in the late nineteenth century. They can now sell everything from kitchen and housewares to clothes, makeup, jewelry, and almost everything a woman loves.

As Avon's sales plan continued to prosper, many other entrepreneurs looked to implement a similar strategy with other products. Carl Rehnborg, a salesman who spent a decade in China (from 1917 to 1927) stumbled on an idea that was to revolutionize both the direct sales and wellness industries. Rehnborg took note of the effects of malnutrition and a poor diet on health while in Shanghai and was convinced that proper supplementation in the form of a multivitamin/multimineral solution was the answer.

 Essential

Network marketing has become an enormous industry, with more than $178 billion in sales in 2013 and no plans of slowing down in the coming years. The Direct Selling Association estimates that approximately 50,000 Americans begin a part-time, home-based network-marketing business each week. This influx of new distributors and customers has helped spiral many of these companies to more than a billion dollars in annual revenue.

He returned to the United States and began to study the relationship between health and nutrition and learned that there were many plant-based substances critical to the human diet. After years of research, Rehnborg formulated the unique product he was looking for, and in 1934 the California Vitamin Company began manufacturing the world's first multivitamin supplement. The name of the product and the company was changed to Nutrilite in 1939.

Rehnborg's wife suggested that in order to better distribute his product he should set up his own sales force consisting of people who were presently happy, enthusiastic customers. The idea worked so well that Rehnborg found himself immersed in training and supporting his sales staff rather than being focused on managing the business.

It was at this point that two of his best sales reps, Lee Mytinger and William Casselberry, sat down with Rehnborg and hashed out the very first "multilevel" sales plan. The idea was simple: If a representative was able to obtain at least twenty-five customers, he was then approved to find his own sales representatives. Once this team reached a total of 150 customers, the "direct" rep was entitled to an additional 2 percent of the sales volume of the group.

Nobody was intrigued by this new strategy more than Jay Van Andel and Rich DeVos, friends who had spent most of their lives together in high school, the military, and in sales jobs. They were passionate about Nutrilite, but after building a considerable team they became concerned regarding talk of the instability of the company. Van Andel and DeVos made the decision to take the multilevel idea and apply it to a company of their own. In April 1959, through consultation and agreement with their group leaders, Van Andel and DeVos formed the American Way Association, later shortened to Amway.

 Fact

Amway eventually purchased the Nutrilite brand and made it a part of its product line. A partial purchase was made in 1972 and full ownership occurred in 1994.

The multilevel plan and marketing strategies instigated by Amway are today utilized in companies all over the world. Almost every network marketing company that exists today stands on the shoulders of what is referred to as the grandfather of the industry. Amway helped not only set the stage for network marketing's present-day success, but the company fought off many legal challenges to the network marketing structure and direct-selling practices, protecting the rights of reps to pursue free enterprise through network marketing.

Common Misconceptions

Network marketing has occasionally had a negative reputation during its existence, much of it perhaps undeserved. A combination of unethical activity by independent distributors or corporate executives, along with the unfortunate timing of developing in a period when illegal pyramid and Ponzi schemes rapidly increased, helped fuel many of these misconceptions and allegations.

With the correct business model, network marketing is an ethical and fair way of growing a business. A genuine company will follow the business and tax laws that apply to its country of operation, and will observe and enforce the compliance laws necessary for its reps to operate within the boundaries of those laws.

In the United States, government organizations such as the Federal Trade Commission and Food and Drug Administration keep a close eye on the way network marketing companies operate and the products—particularly health-related ones—that are sold through every company.

The Australian Therapeutic Goods Administration (TGA) monitors all wellness products sold via network marketing in that country and is widely known as one of the most rigorous in the world. While their standards are seen by some as being overly severe, it helps to know that the products that pass the guidelines set by the TGA help make sure you are using a product that has been examined thoroughly and approved for your use.

 Fact

Approximately 200 companies are currently members of the DSA, with every member pledging to abide by its Code of Ethics and standards in order to become and continue as a member.

The Direct Selling Association (DSA) also plays a significant role in helping network marketing companies abide by agreements in how they handle distributor relations. The DSA is a membership-based organization that helps support its members and advocates for network marketing and direct selling within the community. There is also a one-year probation period for any company that applies before it can officially be a member. This is to ensure that the company is legitimate and follows all the rules. When looking into a company, check to be sure it has applied for or is a member of the Direct Selling Association.

The industry itself has also formed its own watchdogs and overseers. The Association of Network Marketing Professionals meets yearly to discuss matters related to the future and betterment of the industry, and independent analysts such as Rod Cook, Len Clements, and Troy Dooly spend considerable time reviewing and commenting on events and company activities within the network marketing space.

 Essential

Be careful when judging the industry or a company by the actions of an independent representative. There have been many times when representatives have acted outside the terms of their agreement, giving an undeserved bad name to their company.

So let's take a closer look at some of the most common misconceptions and determine what are the facts and what is fiction.

Network Marketing Is a Pyramid Scheme

Perhaps the most common, most misunderstood belief is that legitimate network marketing is essentially an illegal pyramid scheme. As a network marketer, you may find this to be the first objection you hear from prospects. You will have to learn to deal with the fact that many people fear being caught up in a pyramid scheme.

While a network marketing program may sound similar to a pyramid scheme, there is one major difference: Network marketing provides a service or product that is used by an end consumer. A pyramid scheme is simply a money game, where funds are handed through a chain of people until the next person who rises to the top of the pyramid gets paid the accumulated contributions and goes back to the bottom, ready to entice others to participate. Genuine network marketing companies market a product or service through a chain of distributors or reps, but your income is not earned by getting to the top of a pyramid. Your income can only be earned by creating an organization of happy product users and promoters.

 Alert

If you're asked to put forward an investment without any product or service in return, but are told you're in a network marketing business, do your research. Many pyramid schemes try to disguise themselves as network marketing programs.

Dave Ramsey, one of America's most popular and respected financial advisers, recently stated: "Multilevel marketing, network marketing, and direct sales are the names used by those in that type of company to describe how their business model works. These companies are *not* pyramid schemes; they are a legitimate method for some people to make some side money and sometimes to literally build their own business."

Network Marketing Is a Get-Rich-Quick Scheme

While it is definitely not a get-rich-quick scheme, many people view network marketing as a way to create wealth faster. Since the opportunity to grow your business as rapidly and as large as you possibly can is present, there is no doubt that the opportunity to create wealth is available to you. Just be aware that getting wealthy in this business takes the same commitment as with any other business. You'll need to put in the time and effort in order to reap the rewards. There are no shortcuts.

It Takes a Lot of Money to Get Started

Almost every legitimate network marketing company in operation has starting options that would fit into any budget. These options range from under $100 to $2,500. The average starting cost for a network marketing business today is around $500–$800. This first investment often covers a starter kit, marketing tools, an initial product order, and access to online tools, not to mention the support available through your upline and the company itself. The company then handles delivering product, keeping track of your organization, organizing training events, and keeping you up-to-date through regular communication. You get a lot for the investment you have made. When you consider the costs incurred by starting most major franchises or businesses today, the price of getting involved in network marketing is extremely reasonable.

You Can Make a Lot of Money by Doing Next to Nothing

This may be a marketing ploy to get you signed up, but you can be sure that doing nothing after you are in the system will also earn you nothing. This business is not a get-rich-quick scheme. It offers no free rides. You get out what you put in, and in the beginning that can seem like a lot. It takes a lot of effort and patience to grow a team and your income. Sitting on your hands and hoping your business will grow without effort is not a game plan.

You Have to Sell to Friends and Family

You can sell to friends and family, and if the products are that good, you should. But the notion that you will be spending a large part of your time convincing family and friends to buy from you is an outdated one. Many of today's sales techniques revolve around conversationally marketing the product, mentioning it almost casually during normal banter with your friends and family.

For example, if you are marketing a weight-loss product, your own results will show for themselves and have others interested in what you are using. You can then use the company's videos or online resources to help share your excitement. If you are using a service that saves you money, you can casually mention it to your friends and allow them to ask for more information rather than you harassing them to sign on with your company.

The bottom line is the days of begging family and friends to buy from you are long gone. Product results will often speak for themselves, and exceptional marketing material provided by your company is all you need to stir an interest with the people you know.

Only the People at the Top Make Money

A hangover from illegitimate pyramid schemes, the view that only those who get in first make the big money is no longer applicable with today's compensation plans. Plans are now structured so anybody entering the business at any stage can earn as much or even more than a rep who has been working with the company since its pre-launch period.

Positioning and timing still play an important role, but they won't benefit you if you simply take a position in an organization and fail to do what is required to build a business—selling product, creating sales volume, and developing an organization. If you are not focused on these key areas, a new rep who enters the business five years from today will out-earn you.

Network Marketing Is a Cult

In the late '70s and early '80s, the industry entered a new phase. Leaders within many of the major companies began to look for ways to help keep reps from quitting due to the difficulties of developing such an unconventional business. Many reps found it difficult to stay upbeat as they dealt with rejection and reluctant prospects. Company owners and upline leaders were struggling to find an answer. But not for long. The marriage between network marketing and the personal development industry became the perfect match.

Books such as *Think and Grow Rich* by Napoleon Hill, *The Magic of Thinking Big* by Dr. David J. Schwartz, and almost anything written by Og Mandino were now featured at network marketing companies' conventions and training events. Today, *How Successful People Think* by John C. Maxwell and *The 7 Habits of Highly Effective People* by Stephen R. Covey are also among the books that network marketing companies recommend to their reps. A shift from training reps in sales and marketing skills to working on their mindset and attitude proved to be a winning strategy. Positive, upbeat reps are willing to do whatever it takes to achieve their dream, overcome their limitations, and take their opportunities.

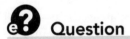 **Question**

Can I still build a network if I'm not interested in personal development?
Of course you can, and for many years personal development played almost no role in the industry. As long as you work to create sales volume, you can be successful. Personal development just increases your potential for the greatest success possible.

At the same time, many large network marketing companies began to dictate dress and behavior codes to their associates and encouraged reps to stay away from family and friends who didn't support their new career and outlook. At a time when most people were unfamiliar with personal development programs, and a friend or relative suddenly exhibited a personality change and began avoiding friends and family, it wasn't uncommon for suspicions or fears to arise. As a result, some people began to theorize that these companies were cult-like. Today, more people are aware of training programs that focus on self-esteem, a positive image, and self-actualization, and the cult comparison is diminishing.

The Market Will Quickly Become Saturated

According to the saturation theory, if a network marketing company works the way it should, every person on the planet will be a distributor or rep within months and there will be nobody left to recruit or sell products to. While that sounds possible theoretically, there are several reasons that this is unlikely to happen.

The first reason is that, quite simply, not everyone will be interested in your business or product. No matter what you do or say, there are people who will find no need to be part of your team. That leaves a huge section of the population out of the equation. The second is the fact that there are millions of babies born every year, which in turn means that eighteen years later they are fresh candidates for a network marketing business. There are more births occurring every year than the number of people joining network marketing, so the possibility of selling to everyone is extremely remote. And finally, many people try this business for a short time and then, for various reasons, move on to other things. Not everyone is suited to this type of business, so there will always be openings for people who are receptive to a career in network marketing.

CHAPTER 3

Network Marketing and Franchising

Some companies sell products through retail outlets, others use direct-mail catalogs, many utilize online stores, and still others rely on professional salespeople. By contrast, network marketing companies have independent reps who work part-time to promote products and services directly to potential customers. These reps are rewarded financially and are encouraged to grow a team to reach higher sales volumes. It is a distinct type of business, with aspects unlike most other endeavors.

The Premise of Network Marketing

The principle behind network marketing is that you will earn an income for creating sales through a network of people who are either reps or customers. You are not getting paid for other people's work, as is often assumed, but only for their ability to create volume through the sales of a product or service to an end user. No matter how many hours your team puts in or presentations they make, if no product is moved to an end consumer, no income can be earned.

When someone in your network makes a sale or purchases items for his own personal use, the volume created by those purchases is accumulated within a certain period, usually weekly or monthly, and you will earn a commission based on that volume. The percentage you are paid will usually become higher as you rise up the compensation plan, which occurs as you create larger volume. These percentages often range from 5–20 percent, depending on the company. Choosing a higher-percentage payout is not always a better option, since other parts of a plan could offset a lower-percentage payout.

You should also be aware that whatever this percentage is, it is not the full amount you may be entitled to. Most companies return anywhere from 40–60 percent of sales generated back to the reps as commission. This means that while one part of a plan may pay you a basic percentage of sales, there are other bonuses and incentives that can potentially be paid to you. These vary from plan to plan and company to company, so you must be sure to understand what these bonuses are in order to take full advantage of them.

 Alert

> Be aware of anyone who tells you that you'll instantly make a fortune just by signing up or recruiting a few people. As with any business, it takes time to establish a customer base and develop a significant income. Recruiters who use this strategy simply want to take advantage of the gullible. Don't be one of them.

That fact gives you the incentive to actively bring in new reps, and to train and support them as well as you can. This important factor is the driving force behind success in network marketing. You are not paid on the efforts of your team; you are paid on their success. That success becomes greater the more you are willing to work with them, encourage them, and teach them to achieve the goals they have set.

Direct-to-Consumer Selling

For hundreds of years, the idea of making or growing a product and then selling it directly to the user was a convention of every economy. As the world of commerce evolved, salespeople began to look at more effective and profitable ways to get their products into the hands of buyers. Corner stores and larger department stores appeared all over the country, housing all the goods a customer could want, and salespeople were no longer required to travel from door to door and city to city to make a sale.

The consumer was able to approach salespeople rather than the other way around. Mail-order catalog sales through Montgomery Ward, Hammacher Schlemmer, and Sears thrived during the early twentieth century as the public took to the novelty of ordering the item of their choice and having it delivered directly to their door.

 Alert

Don't let yourself be convinced to join the next big thing because you feel everyone else is jumping on board. If you don't see yourself actually using the product or comfortably promoting it, you probably won't go far no matter how many others are succeeding with that company.

During this period, shopping malls began to dot the American landscape, offering shoppers an almost unlimited variety of products and services to choose from in one accessible location. Madison Avenue, the mecca of advertising and marketing in New York City, wasted no time guiding people as to what they needed, where to get it, and what color they should ask for. Consumers wanted to keep up with the latest in material goods, and manufacturers and retailers were only too happy to oblige. An industry within the industry materialized, with the warehousing and transport industries barely able to stay ahead of the surge.

As the cost of bringing goods to the market increased, the consequence to consumers was a sharp rise in retail prices. Traders had no option but to pass the higher costs to the end user. If an item cost $10 to manufacture, it was reaching the shelves at Walmart with a $30 price tag. While customers were acutely aware of this price discrepancy, the benefits of having so much variety and choice seemed to outweigh what many rationalized as a minor concern.

At this time, direct sellers and network marketing institutions such as Avon, Mary Kay, Fuller Brush, Wachters, and Amway found a niche in a market where consumers began to value product recommendations from trusted friends and the opportunity to evaluate merchandise in the comfort of their own home before deciding to spend money.

The benefit of buying directly from the manufacturer became a major rallying point. Consumers once again began to see the benefits of buying direct and looked for companies that would deliver goods directly to them, whether it was skin-care products (Mary Kay, Avon, and Nu Skin), personal-care products (Herbalife, Nature's Sunshine Products, and Forever Living Products), or electrical and white goods (Amway and Vorwerk). Network marketing companies were at the forefront of selling direct to the consumer, and buyers were eager to take advantage of both the pricing and superior customer service.

The Internet Effect

Almost no authority could have predicted the true impact the Internet would play in the world of retail sales. Consumers were treated to a barrage of online stores emerging almost daily, more than willing to provide goods and services at wholesale prices with direct-to-your-door delivery. Amazon, eBay, and Zappos.com began to dominate sales in the new medium, with consumers relishing the opportunity to buy direct from these wholesalers even when they had neither tried nor tested the product.

Many brick-and-mortar retail outlets launched online virtual stores in order to compete, and network marketing companies also began to look at how they too could profit from the Internet revolution. In fact, it could be argued that no other business model was so right for the online world. With a direct-to-customer system already a major factor in network marketing, the marriage between online selling and network marketing was practically inevitable.

Today almost every network marketing company allows both reps and retail customers to order directly from the company's website, process payments, facilitate order adjustments, and have the product delivered directly to your door, direct from the manufacturer.

Party-Plan Selling

When Stanley Home Products sales agent Brownie Wise altered her strategy promoting Tupperware in the 1950s, she surely would never have imagined the role she would play in the history of direct selling. Wise began to increase her sales with her home-party approach, and Tupperware's founder Earl Tupper was duly impressed. He invited her to join the company as vice president, and urged her to teach her ingenious system to women eager to supplement their income or to create one.

 Fact

Sony Pictures is currently producing a feature film depicting Brownie Wise's life and how she made famous the Tupperware brand. As of writing, Sandra Bullock has been chosen to play the part of Brownie.

The party-plan system thrived, with women delighting in the opportunity to mix with friends, make new ones, and earn a nice income to boot. As party-plan selling became more popular, companies such as The Pampered Chef, Discovery Toys, and the Longaberger Company entered the arena, and everything from cooking utensils to hand-woven baskets, candles, and lingerie were made available over an afternoon shopping at home with friends.

The basic technique used to grow a party-plan business is essentially the same for most companies that use this format. It will often begin with an enthusiastic invitation to come to a friend's home and help support her new business by taking a look at a new selection of jewelry or makeup. A consultant, or sales representative, will be on hand to support the host of the party, present the products, and encourage sales. A bonus or special discount is often on offer for the host so she is motivated to invite more of her friends to the party.

A professional display, samples, and a demonstration of the products will be offered, and guests will be enticed to purchase items on the spot with special discounts and deals. Finally, a suggestion will be made to all in attendance to hold a party at home, supported by the consultant and the host.

 Alert

If you aren't naturally sociable or comfortable in making new friends, you may find it difficult to succeed with this type of direct selling. Successful party-plan consultants are often outgoing, bubbly characters who find it easy to mix with new people.

While party-plan selling has proved enormously successful, many consultants began to tire of the demands in generating a reasonable income. Long hours on the road, unreliable hosts, and less-than-successful parties had party-plan reps closely examining another direct-sales option—network marketing.

While party-plan consultants were able to profit from their own sales and the sales of their immediate consultants, network marketers were reaping the rewards of reps several levels deep into their plan. You could sponsor Bernard, who sponsors Matt, who in turn brings in Jane-Marie, who then introduces the business to Maria and Kamie. And if Kamie, who is four or five generations deep, was making a sale, there was a better than even chance you would be receiving some sort of commission from her sales.

This point of difference saw many party-plan companies lose consultants to what appeared to be a more rewarding and fairer system. To counter a dwindling share of what was already a niche market, party-plan operators slowly introduced enhancements borrowed from network marketing into their own plans, which helped increase retention and re-energize what had become an integral feature of the free enterprise economy.

Network Marketing— The People's Franchise?

Franchising is a system where a business or government authority issues you an agreement or license to operate in its name. There is a set of standards and method of operation that you are expected to abide by.

There are thousands of franchises available today, providing everything from fast food to car mufflers to accounting services. McDonald's, Jack in the Box, and Anytime Fitness are just three successful franchises out of the many that an aspiring business owner can go into.

Many people will look into franchise opportunities when they consider working for themselves. By buying a franchise, you buy the right to sell a company's products. The company, in turn, provides a well-advertised brand name and very clear guidelines on what you can do and where you can do it. For example, many fast-food franchises demand that you buy all your products from them, that you serve specific items on the menu, and that you use their brand of everything from grill cleaners to napkins.

What Franchises Offer

Franchises typically provide a great deal of assistance in everything from prepaid advertising, ready-made accounting systems, and even how you can go about hiring new employees. However, every piece of assistance provided by the franchiser usually comes with the caveat that you can use only its system or nominated suppliers. For example, if the franchiser provides you with its own advertising, you most likely will not be allowed to create your own. If the franchiser has a preferred company that looks after your equipment, you will only be able to use them and not the plumber or electrician you would usually call.

However, franchises do have some great benefits. First, you get to run the business the way you want on a day-to-day basis. You can hire friends and family members. You can work as many hours as you choose every week instead of hiring someone else. You can even hire a manager and live on the income the franchise brings in.

You also get the profits from the business, so the harder and smarter you work, the better you will do financially. The home corporation usually offers financial incentives such as bonuses and luxury vacations for its top franchise owners and may also have some good retirement programs and benefit packages that you can take advantage of.

Franchise Shortcomings

The conventional business setting of most franchises can be restricting. The people at the home office evaluate your work every year and decide if you are worthy to keep the franchise. If you don't follow its rules to the letter, you could be asked to give it up.

You will no doubt have a lot of restrictions on equipment and supplies, advertising, and location of your business. As a result, many franchise owners end up feeling that the dream of owning their own business is not quite what they thought it would be.

You should also be aware that the initial investment to buy a franchise is quite considerable. Some, such as fast-food franchises, can cost hundreds of thousands of dollars and even up to over a million dollars in some cases. Even simple opportunities, such as a carpet-cleaning business, can carry a hefty price tag of over $50,000 in franchise, equipment, and start-up costs. In addition to the cost of buying the franchise, ongoing license renewal fees have to be considered. Some may charge a monthly or yearly flat fee or a sliding fee based on your revenues or other factors for a set number of years. Others require you to pay royalties on your revenues as long as you stay in business. Many require you to pay a maintenance fee that covers items such as advertising and marketing.

The Network Marketing Difference

Network marketing applies many of the same concepts it takes to grow a franchise, without the high price tag and restrictions that make franchising unattainable for most. A network marketing business will usually cost between $500 and $2,000 to start up, and often includes your initial product order, a starter kit, and access to company and distributor support. Network marketers are free to work wherever they have access to a phone and the Internet, and are not weighed down by having to remain in a location chosen by the company or staying open with hours set by a head corporation. Network marketing companies will often give you guidelines as to what you should comply with in your marketing, then leave you to put in your own creative efforts in producing the advertising that fits in with your message.

Another major difference between network marketing and franchising is the networker's freedom in growing her business in many locations, including overseas markets. A franchise owner is often limited to sales from customers that live within the vicinity of the store. In network marketing, you can live in Milwaukee and have a new customer in Malaysia. As long as the company you are with is open in that country, you can build a business and develop customers in that market.

 Question

What if I have no idea how to create a marketing message?
No problem, that's where your sponsor or company can step in. They will often have tried-and-true advertising and marketing tools ready for you to use or can tailor the materials to what you need.

The key similarity between the two opportunities is the turnkey factor that appeals to those looking at a business for the first time. You won't need to create and manufacture the product, establish a distribution system, or focus on brand recognition. Most, even all, of these areas have been handled by the company and are provided for you to work with. This leaves you with the opportunity to then focus on increasing sales and customer retention.

Network Marketing or Franchising: What Will Work for You?

You may have the available capital and desire to enter a franchise, but you must then decide whether you are ready to commit to a business that you may not have a lot of control over. If you're seeking a lot of freedom and creative input into your business, franchising may not be the answer.

You'll need to be focused on staying within company guidelines and expectations. There may be decisions the franchiser makes, such as placing another franchise close to yours, which you may be unable to do anything about. If you have a thriving Mexican food franchise and you are the only one in your suburb, you definitely don't want a competing store a mile or two down the road. It has happened with many franchise businesses in the past and is bound to have an impact on your earnings.

If, however, the benefits of being part of a system that has shown prior success and offers greater security in terms of brand awareness and financial backing is what you are looking for, then franchising could be your answer.

If not, then network marketing presents you with what could be the perfect option, what many refer to today as "the people's franchise." The business is relatively inexpensive to start, offers you the support of the company and distributors who have been in the game longer than you, and allows you to begin part-time. Add in the fact that your income through network marketing can be as much or even greater than what you could profit in a franchise, and you'll start to see why so many new entrepreneurs are choosing this industry as their starting point.

CHAPTER 4

How You Will Make Money

Compensation plans can be confusing if you are unfamiliar with network marketing. Every company has a slightly different twist on how it pays its reps. Your sponsor and other reps will probably tell you that their compensation plan is the best there is and that their company is the one creating the most success in the industry. But remember, there are no shortcuts to wealth, even in network marketing. If a plan promises big bucks early on, you'll need to stand back and sort out the hype from the facts.

Compensation Plans

A compensation plan, or pay plan, is the structure that a company puts into place to reward and recognize distributors who create sales for the company. Plans vary with every company, and may have different requirements in order for you to earn your commissions and an achievement title.

 Alert

Network marketing involves real products and services. It can't be an "investment opportunity" that relies on the recruitment of other people to make your money. Any activity that focuses on passing money through a chain of people in the hope of creating a greater return may be construed as an illegal Ponzi or pyramid scheme.

A company will usually include bonuses that encourage reps to become higher achievers, but there are typical components that make a compensation plan fair and reasonable to all. When it comes to your plan, look at the advantages for newcomers as well as how much work it will take to really start making the big dollars.

Most network marketing companies base their compensation plans on one of four pay plan structures:

- Unilevel
- Stairstep breakaway
- Matrix
- Binary

Typically, companies don't use these plans in their original form. Most plans combine aspects of two or more plans to make them more appealing to newcomers and experienced reps alike. Aside from the way a company will structure its payout, you'll need to determine whether the plan implemented by your company is one you are able to operate under. This isn't an easy thing to do, even for the most accomplished networkers. The truth is, there are pros and cons for every plan. It's difficult to tell which factors will help or hinder your business building. You'll find a lot of information in company materials and on the Internet, but don't get bogged down attempting to learn everything about a plan before you get started. You can be successful in any plan as long as you realize that the most important thing you need to do to make money is to create sales volume through new and continued product orders. Let's go through the basic plans so you can get an understanding of how each one is structured.

Unilevel Plan

A unilevel plan is the most common and the simplest of plans. You can sponsor as many frontline people as you want, going as wide in the plan as you choose. Generally, all volume in a unilevel plan up to a certain level is what you get paid on. Unilevel plans will often include "compression," which means that empty spots in the organization where reps may not be building or ordering are automatically filled with the next active rep below them. This can potentially help you qualify for higher commissions if your plan allows for it.

One common shortcoming to this plan is that it is usually limits how deep you can build your team. If the plan pays down eight generations, the orders from those in the ninth do not form part of your commission. If a solid leader happens to come in below those levels, you could potentially miss out on the sales volume they create. Morinda (Tahitian Noni), Xango, and Unicity are some companies that use a form of the unilevel plan.

Stairstep Breakaway Plan

The stairstep breakaway plan is the oldest type of compensation plan, and it's rarely used by new companies. In this type of plan, as your reps move higher in the structure, they eventually break away from you and work directly for the company. To compensate for this, the company pays you a monthly bonus as long as the breakaway rep fulfills his volume requirements. In almost all of these plans, the accumulation of breakaway reps is a crucial part of gaining rank advancements. You can sponsor as wide as you want in a stairstep plan, and are usually paid on the whole volume in your organization no matter how deep you build, as long as the group has not broken away. Amway, Nu Skin, and Herbalife are companies that use a form of the stairstep breakaway plan.

Matrix Plan

The matrix plan is characterized by its limited width and depth. Matrix plans are often three levels wide and six levels deep, meaning you can have three team members on your first level, and everyone that follows is placed into a matrix six levels deep. One of the most appealing features of this plan is the benefit of spillover, when team members sponsored by a leader above you are placed into your team. If these new reps prove to be successful, you will benefit from their success with an increase in your commission. The spillover factor, however, has not always proved positive. Some team members may sit back and, rather than work to build a team themselves, expect reps to be placed in their groups from business builders above them. Ingreso Cybernetico, Skinny Body Care, and Melaleuca are companies that use a form of the matrix plan.

Binary Plan

The binary plan features a limited frontline of two reps. Everyone else you sponsor will fall in either of these two legs in the next available open position. This plan also often creates spillover and generates greater teamwork as members are more easily grouped in the same leg.

 Alert

> Be wary of anybody who promises to build your business for you by placing reps in your group with the binary plan. While in some plans this may happen by default, stay clear of promises assuring you of reward for no effort.

While it is often easier to feel a sense of momentum and rapid growth in a binary, the perceived need to be in a "power leg," where a heavy hitter is placing new reps in the tree to the benefit of all in the line, is often cited as one of the reasons people are wary of the binary plan. Not being in this power leg could play a role in your eventual success, although you should never count on spillover or your upline building your business for your success. Isagenix International, USANA, and Team Beachbody all use a form of the binary plan.

Evaluating Your Compensation Plan

No matter what business a company is in, it needs some money to pay its executives, buy or produce the product, pay bills generated by the home office, run marketing programs, and develop new products. Companies frequently put about 50 percent of their profits into operating costs and to reinvest in the company's growth. (This number may vary, as long as it's not less than 30 percent or more than 70 percent.)

To figure out if your company pays a reasonable amount to its reps, tally up exactly how much could possibly be taken from one sale. Figure everyone's cut all the way down the line. If the company is giving more than 70 percent of every sale to its reps, that's good news for today, but could signal trouble in the future, because the company won't have the money to support expansion. If it gives less than 30 percent to its reps, you have to question where the rest of that money is going.

Fairness to All Reps

A program should offer everyone the opportunity to succeed, no matter where they enter the downline. Step back and ask yourself how much you reasonably could sell in a month. Now divide that in half. (No matter how conservative we are, we have a tendency to be too optimistic about the sales, especially in the beginning.) What is your compensation on that half starting today? Does it seem fair for the amount of work you will be putting in?

Many companies give you a guaranteed percentage on sales that can be as high as 40 percent. This means that you receive $4 out of every $10 you make on a sale. It also means that an item that lists for $10 in your catalog really only costs you $6 if you buy it for personal use. This is especially important if you are working for a company that has a number of products you personally use. You may just find that you save enough on your own purchases to justify being a distributor.

You are the only person who can judge the fairness for the amount of work. If you really like to meet people and sell product and you hate your current job, making the equivalent of $6 an hour isn't too bad. If you're looking at this opportunity as a way to become financially independent, you will want to set your sights a little higher.

Ideally, you should expect to get at least $30 an hour for the time you put into the business right from the start. That means if you spend two hours at a sales party, your commission for the sales at that event should be at least $60.

The Downline Bonus

Most companies offer some type of incentive to recruit downline members, although this can vary widely based on the company's marketing plan. Does the compensation plan seem fair? Obviously it takes more work to recruit someone than it does to make a sale. Do you get a bonus for all your hard work?

 Essential

You should receive some type of compensation for bringing in a new recruit. If you don't, make sure that you receive a large commission on your frontline recruit's sales. It should be no less than 5 percent lower than your commission on your own sales.

Some companies choose to give a non-monetary reward for recruiting new reps. The reward usually gets bigger with every distributor you recruit and often can be accumulated, like points, over the course of one or more years. For example, one company gives 100 points for every rep you have recruited. They issue a catalog of luxury products such as computers, televisions, trips, and jewelry. The points can be saved up and used to "buy" those items.

Motivation Potential

The program should be motivating at all levels. Anyone entering at any point in the network should be encouraged to work hard. The standard compensation plan will be motivating if you see it as fair. However, you also want to look for extra motivation. Does the company offer an annual or quarterly contest where top producers can earn trips, cars, or other luxury items? Are there bonuses when you reach certain levels? Take into account the amount of work you need to do to reach the next level of compensation. Are the steps short enough that it's easily reachable, at least in the beginning? Ask your potential sponsor how long it took her to attain the various levels in the program.

Also look for daily motivators that aren't part of the formal compensation plan. The company should respect its reps and stay in contact with them, telling them of anything good or bad happening to the company. Look for little things such as a newsletter for reps, an annual gathering for all reps, regional parties, and even motivational tactics such as letters from the home office when you do well or a supply of "You Can Do It" stickers to place on your bathroom mirrors. All of these belong to the non-monetary compensation category and are definitely important to your morale and long-term commitment.

Reasonable Expectations

The program shouldn't expect too much in terms of sales. Many companies encourage sales by setting the initial compensation very high, from 25–40 percent of the sale. This lets you see success right away. Other companies don't pay much of anything until your sales reach a certain level, such as $1,000 a month. That can be motivating, but also unrealistic and discouraging. Imagine putting in a great deal of work to learn the product and sales strategies only to get a few pennies from every sale. Sure, the company tells you that you can make big money after you hit various goals, but if you realistically can't reach these goals for several years, something is wrong with the goals.

Ask the company how many of their new reps reach that goal within three months. Also ask how many quit before they ever reach it. Ask your sponsor how long it took him and how much work it took. The answers should give you a good indication of how reasonable the company's expectations are.

Volume Requirements

Some organizations require that you (and your downline) purchase a certain amount of product every month. If you fail to meet that limit, you are penalized or even dropped from the ranks, often without being reimbursed for items that you might have purchased.

The volume requirement should be reasonable for you to make in a bad month. Many companies set it at the amount a good, loyal customer might buy in a month. For example, if you sell nutritional supplements and the company has discovered that its best customers spend $100 a month, it's not unreasonable for them to set that as your volume requirement, because you should be able to spend that for your personal use.

Advantages for Newcomers

Some organizations offer advantages for the new distributors, giving them a few months of extra bonus money or bonuses for their first few downline members. Some will even "seed" your prospect list by giving you a few customers from the person at the top of your upline. The idea is to have you see success right away so you are motivated to reach that level through hard work. There aren't too many disadvantages to such an option, except that you have to remember it will go away.

 Alert

There is no magic to finding the right compensation program, and the program shouldn't seem magical, either. If it seems as though it's extremely easy to make big money, you're likely missing something. If it seems like the work is reasonable, you have probably found a solid business opportunity.

The Realistic Middle Level

We'd all like to become millionaires, but what will you realistically make in the program? Find out what the typical distributor is making. How big is the typical downline? If you work a forty-hour week, how much can you expect to be making after a year?

Be wary because most companies and sponsors like to tout the best examples. Remember to look realistically at your own situation—your sales knowledge and experience as well as the product's saturation in your geographic area—to determine how well you might do. Then determine if you can live with that. After all, not everyone can become a millionaire, even if we work hard at it. Can you accept making the more realistic middle level of income?

What Is the Top?

Is there a cap on the program? It may seem far-fetched today, but if the program lets your distributors break away after they reach a certain level, you could see your retirement income fall away just because you found some great distributors. Other programs stop giving you commission at a relatively early level in the downline, such as the fourth generation. Still others begin compensating you with company stock instead of money long before you reach the million-dollar mark. Don't always trust the company's sales sheet. Ask to talk to people who have made it big. Are there many of them, and are there new ones added to the group every year?

The Benefits of Immediate and Residual Income

A compensation plan should allow you to build a business with passive income—money that is paid to you every month, even when no new team members or customers join your organization. The income you will earn is based on ongoing orders from those who were customers in the past and are regularly ordering product or using services every month whether you remind them or not. This is one of the biggest advantages of the network marketing structure. Ongoing orders from long-term customers and representatives continue to be made even when you are taking a break from the business or traveling around the world on vacation or supporting your team.

Companies are continuously working on ways to provide rewards for results, which creates an exciting income opportunity for both part-time and full-time network marketers. In fact, you may be working your business part-time for just an hour a day from home and eventually find that your networking income has exceeded your full-time income through your job. When this happens, it's time to decide whether you want to turn your network marketing business into a full-time endeavor.

Immediate Benefits

In network marketing, commissions are available in the short and long term. The early commissions, or transitional income, are helpful for you to keep your business growing in its early stages, while also providing you with funds to help cover the expenses incurred in getting your business off the ground. Many of these bonuses are available to you whenever you fulfill certain activities in the compensation plan.

 Alert

Don't make the mistake of quitting your job early. Your income from your business, especially in the early days, will fluctuate. Stay with the security of your work income until you can regularly bring in up to two or three times your salary every year and it is dependable.

For example, when you sponsor new people or help your team sponsor new people, you might be paid a "first order bonus" or "fast start bonus." This is not a bonus paid on the recruitment of people, but a commission paid on the first orders made by the new people on your team. The amounts will vary according to your company, but with sums of anywhere between $40 to $500 being paid out in first order bonuses, you can begin to see how rapidly new reps are able to make back the cost of their initial investment.

Retail profits also create immediate income. You buy a product at wholesale, sell it a suggested markup, and pocket the difference. If friends and family are supportive of your new business and are willing to try the products, you can easily earn money quickly. This is also a great way for you to get some early product testimonials.

Many companies pay special bonuses for launching your business quickly or hitting specific sales and recruiting targets early on. You might be invited to be part of a "presidents' club," where you might receive product discounts or preferential seating at training events. Early leadership rewards can be offered for creating a certain amount of volume in your first ninety days. While many companies offer these early rewards to keep their sales force motivated and inspired to work their way up the structure, greater rewards and higher commissions are available as you progress to larger group sales volume and the creation of a bigger team.

Network marketing companies reward you for not only helping bring in sales, but for building your business by bringing in new reps and for becoming a leader in the organization. Every company understands that leaders in the field mean more opportunities for growth and an increased profit margin. Luxury car bonuses, European cruise incentives, and leadership retreats to exotic locations such as Phuket in Thailand and Cancún in Mexico are ways that companies recognize and reward leaders and encourage them to stay focused on growing and supporting their team.

 Fact

Amway was one of the first companies to provide their leaders with private retreats, flying them over for a several-day stay in Peter Island, nestled among the British Virgin Islands.

Mary Kay, one of the largest sellers of skin-care and cosmetics products in the industry, has famously awarded a pink Cadillac to its leaders since 1969, and claims that over 100,000 consultants have now received one. Weight-loss and nutritional products supplier ViSalus gained plenty of attention in its early days in 2005 when reps were being rewarded with new BMWs at an almost daily rate. And Utah-based MonaVie did the same when reps who attained the level of Black Diamond were given the opportunity to take ownership of a new Mercedes-Benz.

Residual Benefits
While exciting rewards and trips draw many people to building a business, the greatest incentive for most people is the prospect of creating long-term, secure residual income. For years, authors,

artists, actors, and manufacturers have benefitted from residual income or royalties. For example, Leonardo DiCaprio starred in the movie *Titanic* in 1997. He made that movie almost twenty years ago, but he continues to earn a residual payment every time the movie is screened around the world. J.K. Rowling finished writing the Harry Potter books years ago, but she continues to earn a residual income on the millions of copies that are still sold today. These aren't typical instances, of course, but they do highlight the power of residual income: Do something once, do it well, and continue to get paid over and over again.

Now, you may be thinking, why is passive income so much more powerful than simply earning a substantial salary or wages? The answer lies in this one undeniable fact—we all have only twenty-four hours in a day. If you only produce an income based on hours worked in exchange for dollars, you've instantly put a cap on what you can possibly earn. And even if you are paid per activity, such as a plumber or architect, your potential income is still limited by two things: maximum hours in the day you can possibly work, and how much you can put in before your body and mind cry "Enough!" Passive income allows you the leverage to break through these unavoidable limits we all live with, which in turn frees up your time and increases your earning power.

 Essential

Your company will use interesting and enterprising ways to dress up its compensation plan, but you should take the time to study each feature and think of it as something you are excited about. If the rewards, over and above money, aren't anything that appeals to you, you will find it hard to get motivated to reach the higher levels.

What would happen if you developed a residual income that was equal or even above your current income? If you are earning

$600 a week right now, what would you do if another $600 in residual income came in on top of what you already make? Would you continue to fight traffic every morning to work? Would you stick with a job that gave you no emotional satisfaction? Would you travel more? Could you renovate your home or buy a larger one? These options and many more become available to you when both time and money are no longer an obstacle. The key to much of this freedom is the creation of residual income.

Most of us will unfortunately never become professional actors, authors, or musicians, so developing residual income through royalties is not something that we can consider as an option. With so many possibilities unavailable to most, network marketing is a viable strategy for the everyday person who does not have the capital, skill, or knowledge to take advantage of other residual income opportunities. In fact, it is an option thousands of families, entrepreneurs, and retirees are turning to in massive numbers, eager to take control of their financial future.

CHAPTER 5

Is Network Marketing Right for You?

It's been said that network marketing is right for everybody, but not everybody is right for network marketing. And while that may have some truth to it, don't be reluctant about getting involved because you believe only businesspeople get involved in network marketing. Anyone can find success in network marketing—college students, stay-at-home parents, and restaurant waiters have all created incredible rags-to-riches stories in network marketing. A general understanding of basic business ideas and a strong desire to learn is more than enough to start with. Let's take a closer look at what you will need to create the results you're looking for.

Is Business Experience Necessary?

You won't need any prior business experience to succeed in network marketing. In fact, some of the largest income earners in the industry are those who have had no experience in being self-employed. Network marketing is an "earn as you learn" business: You can rack up experience and even earn a decent income while still navigating through what it takes to make the business grow.

Network marketing is more about teaching, training, and supporting a team than traditional selling. It's definitely not about convincing people to buy your concentrated laundry soap or selling them on a new phone line when they're totally satisfied with what they presently have. Rather, network marketing is first about sharing the benefits of your products and business to those who are searching for a solution.

If someone is looking for a business opportunity, and when it is in her best interest, share your business with her. If you can talk to people, if you are trainable, and if you can be enthusiastic about helping other people improve the quality of their lives, you can be successful. You don't have to sell people on the business; it involves communicating the same information you have had the chance to look at, and allowing people to make up their own mind as to whether it is for them to take advantage of or not. Ask people to take a look, not buy or join. People can make up their own mind. If they say no, don't take it personally. After all, they are not saying no to you; they are just saying no (or not right now) to the product or the opportunity.

Determining Your Commitment Level

Despite the exaggerated stories that some may use to entice new people to the industry, this isn't a business where you can come in, sponsor a few people, and sit back and count your millions. Network marketing takes a high level of commitment to not only launch successfully but to continue to succeed and develop an income.

 Alert

You will need to commit to overcoming your fears and insecurities. You will need to commit to your team and upline. You'll need to commit to your company. This is not a time to just dip your toe in the water to check if it's okay to dive in. There is only one way to stay afloat in network marketing and that is by immersing yourself in learning and doing what it takes to succeed.

If you are looking at network marketing to help supplement your income, be sure you are prepared to set aside time and money to purchase a starter kit, get hold of the materials necessary to promote your business and products, and then spend time meeting with those who may be open to using your products or joining your team.

To win in this business, you'll need to do more than make a list of ten people who might be interested in what you're selling. You must take into account that the ten on your list may have no interest in being involved or could be planning on joining another network marketing company or business opportunity.

It's easy to get frustrated when this happens, and you may begin to wonder if you are cut out for this work. Even the most resilient, persistent people can find this initial rejection of their business daunting, and in many cases it can be deflating enough for them to quit. If you are easily discouraged, lack the motivation to overcome your fears, and see every obstacle as a major roadblock, your network marketing journey is likely to be a short one.

 Essential

> Don't be surprised to find that some of your friends, family members, or spouse will try to discourage you. They may tell you about people who tried network marketing and failed, and give you all kinds of reasons why it won't work for you. This is when you will be challenged on your commitment level. You'll need to be strong and stay focused on why you got involved. They may not understand why you made your decision, but that shouldn't be a factor in your moving forward. Thank them for their input and stay focused on what is right for you.

If you choose to do this business part-time, you will still need to regularly share and sell product, invite others to join your team, attend local events, and stay updated with company communications. Finding the time may not always be easy, especially when you have a job and a family to look after. But the reward of bringing in that extra income is worth it, and the chance for it to develop into something much greater than you can currently imagine will help keep you motivated and disciplined to make it work.

If you're looking to eventually go full-time, be prepared to do all those things, with the addition of developing your skills, knowledge, and leadership. Travel will be an important factor as your business begins to expand. It's important that your family is aware of why you need to do this and how it helps the business. If you can, get the support and commitment up front from your family members.

Are You Prepared to Work with and Support a Team?

Growing an organization is a team-building exercise. Your goal is to grow the largest team you can, creating as much sales volume you can, until you reach the income goals you have set yourself. There is simply no way you can reach the higher income levels unless you are prepared to help develop and support your own team.

You will receive the help of your upline and company to help make this happen, but primarily it is your role to focus on team development, making sure your team members are aware of what it takes to build their income and reach their own goals.

 Essential

Network marketing has a funny way of paying you very little for a lot of effort in the beginning, then rewarding you greatly with less of an effort from you later on. If you continue to do what is needed to grow an organization, you will begin to see income flowing constantly even though you are not working the business as hard.

You will become a teacher, motivator, inspirer, confidant, and coach. Your team will look to you for leadership and encouragement. Some people find this difficult to adapt to. They've succeeded with most things by working on their own and relying on their own efforts. If you are someone like that, just be open to the possibility that sharing your knowledge and success from the past with people eager to learn from you will bring about an incredible change in you and your perspectives in working with a group of inspired people.

The Financial Investment

Of course, you simply can't build a business without incurring expenses. Most companies offer several start-up options that require various degrees of financial input on your part. Some plans can start as low as just $50, but it's more typical to need to invest at least $100 to start up as a representative, and some organizations require a minimum of $500.

Don't let a high start-up cost scare you, though. First, it's a way the company can make sure you are serious about working the business. It's not uncommon for a company that has a low-end start-up plan to find that people join as reps as a way to buy the product for themselves and have no intention of selling it to others or finding other team members. If you have a bigger investment to recoup, you're more likely to really work the business.

Higher start-up costs usually point to more services that the company provides for you, such as four-color product catalogs or a personal website. You may find that the cost of buying these services later on far exceeds the cost of getting them in the beginning because you can no longer take advantage of the discount packages offered to new recruits.

Before you get started, you will need to think about the parts of your new business venture that will require some kind of investment on your part.

Starter Package

A starter package is usually your first order with a company. Depending on the company, a package could include sample products, catalogs, marketing materials, and information on the support that your new company will provide as you get started. Sometimes a starter kit is no more than a link to a website and access to a corporate office with all the start-up information and materials you'll need. Some companies have no fixed packages to choose from, but allow you to pay a small registration fee followed by an order from the company for any amount of products you choose.

 Alert

Be wary of companies that ask you to invest thousands of dollars in becoming a representative. You should be able to set up your entire business, from start-up kit through office essentials, with less than $1–$2,000, although you may choose to spend more on additional marketing tools.

You should keep in mind that the option of sponsoring new people is not a compulsory part of you becoming a team member. There are reps who join a company and then build a small retail base that brings them in enough of an income to be satisfied with. What you do after you register with the company is your choice and responsibility. Your sponsor and the company will support you in whatever that choice is.

Marketing Material

Your company and upline will have produced professional materials for you to use to help promote and educate your prospects about your company and its products. Much of the company material is often sold at cost or for a small profit in order to encourage reps to make use of them. Using company-made resources means that the information will be in compliance with both company and government requirements. This is especially important if you will be selling health and wellness products.

Events

Company-sponsored events often include information nights or business presentations for those looking at the business for the first time and training events for established reps. Almost every company holds an annual convention, open to all reps. At an annual convention, new products are launched, major incentives are unveiled, and significant company announcements are made.

While business presentations are often held an hour's drive away or less, attending a major event like an annual meeting could require booking a flight and staying in a hotel for a few days. For most people that's not a small investment. However, almost nothing can beat the inspiration you can receive from a regional or national event having spent time with thousands of excited team members ready to take control of their lives!

An event ticket can cost anywhere from $10 for a local business presentation to more than $400 to attend a two- or three-day company convention. Speak to your sponsor about which events you should be aware of and expected costs involved so you can budget for them.

Travel Expenses

As your business grows and your leadership level rises, you may be expected to travel more in order to help either support a new team or attend an event. This won't be a factor if you are focused on simply retailing product and making a few hundred dollars on the side to help increase your income. But if you are looking to build a secure, residual income, you should be prepared to invest some money in getting around to meet with your team members and help boost their growth. Don't feel like you will be living out of a suitcase for weeks on end. That is rarely, if ever, the case. You'll be looking at a total of perhaps seven to ten days of the year at most, with most trips away not lasting more than a couple of days.

Office Expenses

The best part about a home-based business is that you can decide just how much money to spend on creating your personal workspace. You can turn a spare room into an office with actual office furniture, or you can work in your kitchen or dining room. There's no need to start with a state-of-the-art home office, filled with the latest gadgets and expensive stationery. Your smartphone, a computer, and perhaps a printer are more than enough to get you going. Basic items such as pens, a whiteboard and markers, and printing paper should be included in your office. Just remember that you won't be expected to sit and work in your home office all day, nor should you. Keep to the minimum amount of items you will need in order to get started, then add other stationery and equipment when the income from your business allows you to and only if you really feel it is needed.

The Time Investment

Over 90 percent of reps who enter the industry work part-time. They are often working full-time in a job or another business, or could be busy looking after a young family. One of the most notable aspects of network marketing is that you can build an income no matter how much you can invest into it. There are team members succeeding with five hours per week, and there are team members who have two or three days or more per week to invest into growing their business.

Even some of the very highest income earners put no more than fifteen to twenty hours a week into business building. This is simply because network marketing was created as a part-time business. The way it is structured and the tasks involved in growing your business were established for those who have little time but wanted to find a way to leverage it.

 Alert

As you think about working your business, always look for the most efficient way to do something. You work for yourself now. Any time you waste could be time put into helping your team members or following up with a prospect.

As you begin your business, sit down with your sponsor and make it clear as to the hours you can commit and when are the most likely times of the week and month you will be free for business activities. Then be disciplined about sticking with your time-management plan. You will notice, like many before you, that time can slip away very quickly if you are not firm with engaging in business-building activities at the times you have allocated.

The Importance of Being Coachable

Being coachable is a state of mind and attitude. It simply means you are open to being mentored by those more experienced than you so you can more rapidly achieve whatever it is you are aiming for. If you want to accelerate your learning, develop a great income, and start to create financial freedom, it's important that you be open to mentoring and support.

All you will need to do is find one or two people in your company who are successful, and then be coachable enough to follow their example. Network marketing is a business that is built on the idea of coaching and mentoring. You will find that most experienced reps will be open to answering your questions and giving you valuable advice.

Checklist: Is Network Marketing Right for You?

While the benefits of network marketing are highly appealing, the requirements of building this type of business are not for everyone. You will, like most people, be great at some things and need help with others. Or you may have "non-negotiables" in your personal life that could get in the way of building it successfully. It's a good idea to go through this list and be totally candid with yourself about whether network marketing is something you believe you can succeed in.

- ❏ Have you allocated money to invest in starting the business properly with the right tools and starter kit?
- ❏ Are you committed to making a monthly or weekly order of products? Will you pledge to use them yourself?
- ❏ Are you willing to learn the skills needed to promote and market the company's products or services?
- ❏ Are you flexible and resilient enough to deal with unexpected events?
- ❏ Are you ready to make a list of friends, family members, and associates? Are you ready to present your business and products/service to these people knowing that some will reject the offer?
- ❏ Are you committed to overcoming your fears of starting a new business or becoming a salesperson?
- ❏ Are you committed to working with your upline and company?
- ❏ Have you thought about the time it will take to succeed in network marketing, and how you will find five to fifteen hours a week to grow your business?
- ❏ Are you willing to travel if necessary?
- ❏ Do you have the discipline to run a business so that tasks can be done in a timely manner?

- ❏ Are you committed to building your business in the face of possible opposition from family members or friends?
- ❏ Do you consider yourself a team player?
- ❏ Are you prepared to support and encourage your team members?
- ❏ Do you have the patience to stick with your new venture for a period of time before you experience a demonstrable increase in income?
- ❏ Have you budgeted for monthly marketing tools to help promote your product and company?
- ❏ Are you prepared to attend local and national events in order to spend time with other achievers and your own team?
- ❏ Have you allocated a specific space for your home office?
- ❏ Are you willing to be mentored and open to learning from those who have achieved success?

Where there any questions that surprised you? Anything you felt made you uneasy? Or did you go through the list and feel exhilarated by the opportunity that awaits? Make sure you've really thought about your answers, as the list you have just gone through is filled with the very questions you will ask yourself often during your experience, particularly in your initial business building days.

If you're unsure of anything, or feel that you need clarification on certain points, be sure to speak with your upline or a company leader so she can explain exactly what the expectations are within your company and your organization.

CHAPTER 6

Choosing the Right Product or Service

There are three questions that you need to ask yourself when you look at a product or service to promote in network marketing. Would I use the product or service myself? Would I happily endorse this product or service for others to use? Would I use this product or service even if there were no compensation plan attached? When you decide to get involved in network marketing, you need to invest some time in looking for a good product that you can genuinely support and that will help your business to grow.

Research Potential Products

There is no secret to doing good business research. It is just a matter of being thorough and looking into every aspect of the product. In some cases, it is as simple as using common sense. In others, it might take a little research on the Internet or a few phone calls.

No matter how long it takes you, though, doing the research to find a good product is very important. A bad product will quickly frustrate you and could even leave you with liability lawsuits. A good product, on the other hand, will be the cornerstone that grows your business into the future.

Almost anything you can now buy online or through a retail store is bound to also be available through network marketing. And you may be surprised with the range of products that show up and enter the marketplace through network marketing.

The products and services offered through this industry usually offer excellent value for money. If they did not, most companies would fail to survive in what is an exceedingly competitive market. While you can be confident with the quality and demand for most products in this industry, your decision must still be based on a product line you can use, recommend, and make an income with. There has to be a satisfied end user for what you are selling, which includes yourself and members of your circle of friends and family.

A Product You Believe In

According to the Direct Selling Association, the second most common reason people got into network marketing is that they believe the product is good. (The first reason, not surprisingly, is to make money.) You are betting your future on this product, so it's critical that you believe in it. Yes, you can make some sales on an item that you don't believe in, but your attitude will soon catch up with you, and people won't be excited because they will sense your disinterest.

In fact, perhaps the best way to select a company is to look at the products you currently use. If you are totally dedicated to one company's product line, that's likely the one for you. Even if the market is fairly saturated and the product's growth potential isn't the best, you can overcome these barriers with your belief and enthusiasm.

A Product You Understand

In today's world, you can always find a few people who will buy from you on blind faith, but consumer advocates and hard-hitting current affairs programs have made more and more people skeptical about almost everything they purchase. They want to know why a product works and how it works. Even if a product is well established in the marketplace, you will need to answer these questions.

The company that supplies your product can and should give you an explanation of why its products work—but does the explanation make sense? Do you personally understand how protein shakes can help your customer lose weight? Can you explain why antioxidants are essential for the body? Even more important, can you describe this easily and quickly to a customer, or do you find yourself just referring him to a website? If you personally don't understand how and why the product works, you're going to find yourself hindered in trying to grow a solid customer base.

 Essential

Try to explain the product to a ten-year-old child, then ask the child to explain it to someone else. While the child may not remember all the details, the general explanation should match yours. If it works, you know you can explain the complexity of your product to anyone.

You don't have to be a product expert to provide good explanations. They just have to make sense. For example, one company sells pain relief strips that provide heat for aching muscles. Complete textbooks have been written on pain relief, but all you need to know is that heat causes blood to rush to the area, and the increased blood flow relieves the pain.

When Quality Is Key

Perhaps even more difficult to explain is how your product is better in quality than a competing item. You'll also need to clarify why that higher quality even matters. Let's say, for instance, that you are selling skin-care cream. You might tell your prospect that this cream works better than 80 percent of creams on the market because it contains the latest ingredients discovered by cutting-edge research. "That's great," your customer replies, "but I'm a twenty-year-old guy, why should I care? It's going to take years before I start getting wrinkles, and by then something new will come along to erase them all." How do you respond?

You can point out that if he uses the cream now, there's a greater chance he won't develop many of the unsightly wrinkles others his age will be stuck with. It also could mean that even when he gets to the age of fifty, he'll still have the looks of a man half his age.

Another company sells scented candles. Your customer may think all candles are the same. You can then show her that the candles you promote come in a special warmer, which means she has no concerns with an open flame or soot buildup on the walls. Add that to an incredible range of over fifty aromas, fast delivery, and an exceptional returns policy, and you can start to create value in the mind of your customer.

Evaluate the Market

Any good businessperson knows that there must be a market for your product if you're going to make any sales. And even if you plan to spend most of your time recruiting new distributors, product must be sold to someone at some point or no one will make any money.

There is a great deal of leeway within that statement. The more money you make per item, the fewer items you will need to sell. On the other hand, if the item is the type of product that is in frequent use and is easy to sell, such as cleaning supplies, a lower price point per each item can still help you make big profits.

The One-Time Buy

There's a reason that motor vehicles, large appliances, and most electronic items don't work well in network marketing: They are usually purchased once over a several-year period. The business works best when it revolves around a product line or service that can be used daily. Makeup, skin care, nutritional supplements, cell phone service, and electricity are things you use every day without much decision-making. Traditionally, it has been these types of necessities that have succeeded in the industry.

 Alert

You want a product that has a growing audience. For this reason, you likely might choose a company that offers a wide range of items that meet the needs of many different people.

Look for product lines that can grow with the person. If you sell beauty care, for example, the product line should include items that appeal to teenagers, adults, and the elderly. Your customers will gradually change what they order as the years go by, but they will remain loyal to you and your product line.

On the other hand, if your product appeals only to one small group of people—such as those with back pain—you must constantly search out new customers. Granted, there are millions of people who experience some form of back pain, but having a customer continue to buy from you even when the original product he bought is no longer required will help you keep your income steady and predictable.

A Fair Price

Examine the products closely and see how they stack up for price against items in the retail market. Look at the general range of products and see if yours fall somewhere in between the low and high ends. Be careful to look at the quality of the product, because that can significantly change the price. For example, children's educational materials can vary widely in price. If you have definite proof that the item you are considering is high quality, it's fine that it falls toward the high end of the price spectrum.

Possible Product Saturation

Market saturation isn't a problem if you have reason to believe you can break out of your region by recruiting new reps and developing customers in other states or countries. You may have friends and relatives in another state who you are certain would become reps, or you might have hobbies or projects that require you to travel to other parts of your country.

Is the Marketplace Changing?

Many a network marketer has gotten caught in a changing marketplace. A good company will be aware of any changes and alter its product line accordingly. Read online articles in the general area of the product and try to determine what is happening in the industry. Are you thinking of selling a clothing line? Look for which fabrics are popular today or deemed to be an oncoming trend.

 Alert

If the product is totally unique and has no emerging competition, it may be a sign that other manufacturers don't see long-term value in competing. The sign of a good product or idea is that it eventually attracts some competition. The competition doesn't have to be as good as your item, but it should provide a comparable function.

For many years the nutritional-products category in network-marketing company was only providing pills and tablets. Nobody questioned this delivery system or even considered if it was the best approach to provide nutrients to the body. In 1970, Juice Plus+ was one of the very first companies in the industry to begin providing nutrition in a powdered form that could be mixed into a shake. For those who had trouble swallowing pills and capsules, this was a convenient alternative.

Over twenty years later, juices began to enter the network-marketing sphere, filled with exotic fruits, nutrients, and product claims that often edged on the outlandish. In 2005, the nutritional-products category encountered innovation again when Agel introduced suspension gel technology—a delivery format that allowed nutrients to be suspended in a gel, carried in portable sachets.

There will always be revolution and improvements applied to every product category. The industry has often been a category creator, ready to adapt to changes and providing its distributors with what is often seen to be the latest generation of products in many classifications.

Do You Know Your Potential Customers?

The customer is an important part of the decision for virtually any product you might consider. You may have determined that the item has a wide market available, but for some reason you aren't attracted to promoting it. That could be because you aren't comfortable with the people you would be selling to.

For example, if you are a fifty-something man who has no children and has been a diesel mechanic for thirty years, you probably wouldn't want to sell children's toys. These products might be something you can believe in, but you likely wouldn't be comfortable with the young mommies you'd be selling to.

Another example is handwritten cards. Their popularity is still strong across certain demographics. Network marketing companies such as SendOutCards have made it virtually seamless to send out cards. But if you don't enjoy connecting with people and staying in touch with old friends and business associates, you may find the idea pointless and not worth promoting.

Sell to Yourself First

Most people decide to sell to people like themselves. That makes sense, because people like you will probably like the product as much as you do. However, you will also have to break out of your group of friends and relatives into the bigger world. Are you prepared to do that?

Here is an example: When a popular line of kitchen utensils started network marketing, a retired chef living a modest lifestyle in the country decided to become a representative. His first customers were professional and amateur gourmet chefs, and his work ran smoothly.

However, eventually he realized that he needed a larger base of customers. The more typical customer base for the items he was selling turned out to be young urban professionals. It was then that our chef found out that he really didn't like working with these people, and became content with earning a lesser income serving those he had a connection with, rather than dealing with customers he was hesitant in selling to.

 Fact

Remember, you won't enjoy working with everybody. You're bound to have customers you don't seem to get along with. However, you want to make sure that you agree with your typical customer's outlook on life, including his or her morals and values. If you don't, it will quickly show in your sales and enthusiasm.

Looking to Alternatives

At the same time, you may see a big opportunity that other reps for the company have missed. Perhaps you can see that a large segment of people who would be interested in the product line have never been approached about it.

Some houseware reps have made large sales to relatively penniless college students who were starting to think about setting up their own households. One distributor that promoted skin care and makeup went to breast cancer support groups, noting that people in chemotherapy frequently seek ways to look more beautiful. A toy salesperson went to elderly housing complexes and pitched the items as perfect gifts for grandchildren. An herbal remedy salesperson sold to nurses and doctors at her workplace, convincing them that they needed to at least try what their patients were considering.

If you think you might have an alternative customer base for your product, ask a few other reps what they think. Find out if the company has ever approached these groups and what happened. Most importantly, look to these groups for advice. Visit them with product brochures before you make your decision.

Performing a SWOT Analysis

A SWOT analysis evaluates strengths, weaknesses, opportunities, and threats of a particular product. Professional salespeople and marketers frequently perform SWOT analyses when they are trying to decide on their sales or marketing strategies. This same tactic can help you decide if a product is right for you.

Strengths

Strengths can come in many different forms. They can be tangible (the product is available in a sturdy plastic bottle) or intangible (the product has been in use for more than forty years). They can include—but are not limited to—all of the product benefits the parent company likely has supplied you with.

Generally, a strength is anything that makes the item easier to sell. To find the product's strengths, go through all the information you have gathered and decide what might make someone decide to buy this product if all other factors were equal between it and a competing item. In particular, consider the following:

- **A well-known name.** This means you don't have to inform your customers about the product. A proven brand name is generally preferable over an unknown one, even if the unproven product is a better value. This is the reason name-brand groceries sell better than store brands. They're the same item, but people like to buy the name they know.

- **Duration.** The product has been around for several decades. It's apparently versatile and can meet different needs.
- **Performance.** If the product is proven to perform better than all of its competitors in nonbiased scientific studies, there is little to argue with here. Scientific evidence that your product works better than another similar item is very convincing sales information.
- **Price.** If the product is relatively low priced, many people will give it a try—even if they aren't convinced that it's better. If the product is high priced, it might appeal to a smaller group, but you will get a higher commission for each item you manage to sell. Some people want the prestige of buying top-of-the-line products, and it'll be easier to sell high-priced items to them.
- **Quality.** High quality means good value for money. For example, if you can show that your laundry detergent costs twice as much as the supermarket brand but will clean three times as much laundry, you have quality as a strength.
- **Environmentally friendly.** More than ever, consumers are conscious of the environmental impact of their buying decisions, and are acutely aware of the negative effects of man-made chemicals. These people will be interested in purchasing products that are all-natural and have not been tested on animals. And other folks certainly won't see this as a weakness.
- **Packaging.** Packaging makes products look more expensive, so your customers will feel they are getting more value for their money. In addition, you won't have to

deliver damaged boxes to your customers or worry about customers hurting themselves on broken bottles.

- **Media attention.** If the product category is getting a lot of attention in the press, you'll have an easier time educating your customers about the benefits of your item.

Weaknesses

Weaknesses are anything that may make your product more difficult or complicated to sell. Interestingly, what is perceived as a strength in one product can be a weakness in another.

- **A well-known name.** Your customers may have preconceived ideas about the product. If those ideas are negative, you'll have a harder time changing the consumer's mind than if you had to educate him from the beginning. For example, Amway products have proven themselves for over fifty years, but many consumers still have apprehension in regards to purchasing their products.
- **Outdated.** The product has been around for several decades and might be perceived as being old-fashioned and out of date.
- **Price.** If the product is relatively low priced, people might think it lacks quality and is not worth trying. If the product is high priced, people might think it's not worth their money.
- **Value for money.** Most people would be hesitant about splurging $120 on eye cream. But they wouldn't be so bothered with a $30 purchase, easily figuring they can get three for the price of the more expensive version.
- **An innovation.** If the product is new to the marketplace, you will need to educate consumers about it, and you will run into skepticism. You also run the risk that the item won't live up to its claims.

Opportunities

Opportunities are created by what is happening in the market-place, and they make your product easier to sell in the future. Consider these examples of market opportunities:

- **More people are searching for products to boost their energy.** If your product helps workers get over that 2 P.M. slump and avoid high-sugar options in the process, that's a definite opportunity.
- **The population of the United States is growing older.** If you have an item that appeals to a maturing generation, this is a definite opportunity.
- **People are waiting until their thirties to have children.** If you sell expensive toys and educational materials, this is to your advantage because older parents have more disposable income.
- **Your product offers convenience.** People feel like they are busier than ever and are desperate for ways that can help make their life more convenient. They're looking for life hacks, and your product could provide it. Any product that is easy to carry around, isn't time-consuming to prepare, and is easily ordered online goes a long way with what people want in today's society.

Threats

Threats can refer directly to an individual product or to the company. Like opportunities, frequently they are things that could happen in the future. As a result, they often aren't used to make a decision about whether to sell a product (unless there are so many threats that the idea of getting involved becomes absolutely frightening). For the most part, you want to know what the threats are so you can determine if you and the company are equipped to handle them in the event that they occur.

- **The product line is increasingly popular.** Due to this popularity, competitors are springing up every day in all sectors—from direct sales to retail. You and the company will have to fight harder to convince people why your products are a better option.
- **An aging population.** Eventually this will mean that more people are living on fixed incomes, reliant on Social Security and past savings. If you sell things that appeal to a younger generation, you might find this demographic shift plays a substantial role in your selling potential.
- **Your product is viewed as a luxury item.** Jewelry, designer clothing, and overseas travel are things your customers will be thrilled to purchase, but they can often be the first things people cut back on if a recession occurs or your customers have been forced into conservative spending due to a financial setback. Global Wealth Trade (GWT) in Canada entered the niche luxury goods market in 2005. While GWT has prospered in what has been a stable economy, sound management and strong leadership has also overcome any reservations by its customers to keep buying in tougher financial times.
- **The product has no scientific validity.** A consumer group or research company might discover that your product has no evidence it works. If the product fails the examination, your company may be have a tough time staying afloat.
- **The product has been tested on animals, uses man-made chemicals, or is made in a third-world country.** All of these factors can be hot buttons for large groups of people. Unfortunately, these things can become important with very little warning, jumping from a fringe-group interest to the mainstream almost overnight.
- **The product is a service that everyone uses or needs.**

Putting It Together

You can make your SWOT analysis as simple or as detailed as you like. However, the more work you put into it, the more information you will have to help you make a decision about a specific product line.

You will never find the perfect product or service, but you can minimize your risk by spotting major red flags before you join. Learning about the benefits and shortcomings of your product will open your eyes to fresh selling ideas and untapped customer groups.

Search Online for Company Reviews and Product Experiences

An Internet search should come up with at least five entries for the company's name, including articles, the company's home page, and perhaps mentions in industry websites.

Is There a Real Market?

Many products may sound glamorous, but fail to meet expectations. Laundry balls that are meant to wash your clothes better and gas tablets that guarantee more efficient fuel consumption often fall into this category. Others simply never appeal to the public's imagination or interest. Take a gut check and think about whether those you know in your circle of friends and family would be open to using them.

Is the Product Unique or a Less Costly Alternative?

It can be difficult to succeed with a product line that presents no real difference with what is already available from a retail store. Does the company have a product that only it produces, or common items that you already use daily such as personal-care products that are of higher quality and value for money?

Look for a product or service where the benefits of purchasing through your company outweigh buying it from anywhere else.

CHAPTER 7

Choosing the Right Company

It's impossible to choose your product or service without also looking at the company that you would be working with to distribute it. You want your network marketing venture to have a bright future, so you need to make sure the company you align with has your future in mind too. Look for a company that is well established and has a sound reason for selling its items through this method.

Management

Most companies are led by one person, or a partnership, who may extend partial ownership to other executives as the company grows. A few are looking to become public companies in the future and offer opportunities for their reps to gain stock ownership, a strategy that CVSL (formerly Computer Vison Systems Laboratories) introduced to many of its members in 2015.

The ownership status doesn't have great significance unless you find extremely good or bad news. If the company has grown significantly but is still owned by one person, that gives you a sense of its management priorities. If the company is planning to go public and is offering incentives for salespeople to earn stock, that is a definite plus in your potential income column.

If it is a public corporation, you will have access to its annual report as well as other financial documents. All publicly traded companies in the United States must file regular financial reports with the Securities and Exchange Commission (SEC), and updated files can be accessed online (*www.sec.gov*).

If you are looking at a privately held corporation, you may or may not have access to its financial reports, but you will be able to gain a lot of information from the company's website and third-party resources. In some cases, companies can make only certain "top company" lists, like those on the Direct Selling News (*http://directsellingnews.com*) or Business for Home (*http://businessforhome.org*) websites, by providing verifiable evidence of their achievements. The annual report and other financial documents will tell you how much debt the company has and will usually include information on why that debt exists and how the company plans to remain solvent in the future.

 Alert

Gross income is not the best predictor of a company's financial standing. Many wealthy people have filed for bankruptcy, as have many large corporations. Instead, you want to look for clues that determine the company's financial stability, such as paid down debt and an increasing asset base.

In the case of a privately owned company, you could contact the company directly and speak to a regional manager or vice president in regards to the company's current financial position and future plans. A private company isn't obligated to tell you the financial position of the company, but it should be more than open with what it is doing to strengthen its market share.

Once you have discovered the company's administrators and management team (usually listed on the company's website), you will need to do a quick search online to examine any negative or positive reports in regards to their reputation and history. Court cases, particularly those that may involve the CEO or even CFO, will allow you to get a better feel for the type of people running the company. But remember, anyone can file a lawsuit, and all parties should be considered innocent until proven guilty.

 Fact

An Internet search on any major search engine should come up with at least five entries for the company's name, including magazine articles, the company's home page, and perhaps mentions in industry listings.

There are some vital signs that will point to a strong management team. These include:

- **The executive team has spent a reasonable amount of time in the company.** If the CEO changes every eighteen months and management positions revolve like a game of musical chairs, you'll want to work out if the team is stable enough to partner with.
- **The company's leader has a great deal of business experience.** If the president or CEO doesn't have experience with network marketing, he or she should have at least had successful business experience, such as in sales management, where similar skills have been exhibited.
- **People at the top understand network marketing.** They may not have a great deal of experience in the area, but they should know everything there is to know about this business style or are at least are willing to learn.
- **Sales executives in the company have experience in network marketing.** This is the one area where you can't slack off. The sales trainers and support team must know what you are dealing with every day and be prepared to make your life easier with their experience and knowledge.

- **The executives have a broad base of expertise.** Too many network marketing companies are started by someone with a good idea backed by savvy marketing. But beyond that, the business expertise starts to falter. The management team should have a broad base of experience in business areas including marketing, distribution, and product development, as well as in management.

Company Vision and Mission

The company should have a clearly stated vision for its future. You will often find this mission stated on the company's website and in many marketing materials. While a vision may come in a variety of forms, it must encompass the company's growth objective and the plan for getting there. For example, your company might say, "We want to be the world leader in supplying high-quality personalized bags to women through network marketing."

 Alert

You may often hear clichés such as "We want to change the world" or "We want to change the industry." This doesn't give a clear idea as to why the company is in business or what its true overall mission is. A good mission statement will mention what the company produces and how it can help enhance the lives of its customers.

The mission is a more day-to-day tool that is used to help guide the company's employees and reps as they make daily routine decisions. Ideally, any question you have about working the business should be answered by turning to the mission. For example, the same company's mission might be, "To provide high-quality, exceptional-looking personalized handbags at a fair price with timely delivery." That pretty much tells all the staff members what to do and what their attitude should be every minute they are working.

You should be able to get a great deal of information from printed material, websites, your potential sponsor, or from the company directly. This should include detailed product information and general information about the company's history, goals, and structure. You might also obtain information from industry associations such as the Direct Selling Association. These groups frequently produce directories of their members. Some will have lists of companies in various categories such as sales revenue or even association involvement. A truly good company with a truly good product or business philosophy is bound to grab the attention of the media, so there should be at least a small article on the company in some publication. Do an online search to see where, if at all, a company has been mentioned. Steer clear of any companies that have absolutely no publicity.

Do Your Research

Today the Internet and online search engines can rapidly bring you up to speed with testimonials and product research regarding almost anything on the market. Add to that the growing number of regulatory authorities that keep an eye on consumer protection and make sure that products marketed with unsubstantiated claims are forced off the shelves both physically and online.

Of course, if the products you are considering are coming from a friend, it's much easier to simply ask that person for a sample or even to buy some for a trial run. You'll soon know whether the product results are in line with the claims being made.

And don't start promoting anything until you are 100 percent sure there are no major issues when it comes to the safety of the products. Some products related to skin care and nutrition have been known to have adverse effects. You should take the time to find out if there have been any problems reported before you start handing them over to family and friends.

 Alert

This is not the time to be casual about what you are looking to promote. You must evaluate each product on its own merits and in terms of your needs. If you go into a network marketing opportunity without evaluating the products and making sure they have proven, positive results, you could be setting yourself up for some major headaches down the road.

As you do your research, you will find that better products will generally have more information available on them. That's because the company isn't afraid to talk about these items and because the marketplace is genuinely excited about them, whether they are years old or brand new.

Rely on Your Own Experience

The first step in your market analysis is to simply look around and get a feel for the product's potential. Is the product interesting to you? Will you use it on a continuing basis? Does it seem like an item that will be around for a long time, or does it appear to be a passing fad? Do you hear people talking about similar products, and have you read articles in magazines or seen something on Facebook or Instagram about this type of item becoming popular?

Let's take essential oils as an example. It seems like everyone is talking about them, and they are gaining in popularity across the globe. With all the attention on the side effects of prescription drugs, many people are at least mildly interested in them. More and more magazine articles appear on the subject every day. If you can think of several people off the top of your head who might buy them, or who already buy them through a retail store, you can probably proceed to the next step in the product research process.

Ask Your Friends and Family

A good way to evaluate the market for the product is to ask your potential sponsor for company-produced product information and show it to your family and friends. Ask everyone for their opinions about the products, the pricing, and the features and benefits being claimed. Also, ask them what they look for in products like this. For example, if you're looking to sell a line of cutlery products, find out what's more important to your potential customers: Is it the cost, quality, or a warranty? Every person has different reasons for buying something, but you want to know what your future customers are looking for.

 Essential

Don't rush into asking your friends and family to buy from you immediately. Explain that you want their honest opinion of how well the item would sell and whether they might consider buying it.

Contact the Company

The company that wants you to sell its products should be able to tell you about its product line and its sales figures. Ask for written material or online information that can help you determine the products' place and acceptance in the market.

In addition, the company should have information indicating where the product is selling best, particularly related to an age group, sex, and geographic region. Some products could work very well in New York but fail to find a steady market in Texas. You'll want to look into the reasons why and determine whether there is a factor there that could impact your own efforts.

While you won't be an employee of the company, you will want to know that the company pays a good wage and treats its actual employees well, because that is a sign of how it will treat its sales force. You want to know that the company sees you as the most important person in the business. You are the person who brings in the money that pays the top executives and even the janitors at the home office.

Learn about Delivery and Returns

Consider how the company handles the delivery of its products to end users and what the policy is on returns or refunds. Although less common these days, some companies may ship items to their reps, who must then deliver them to their customers. If this is the case, be prepared to spend more time in the car (or at the post office) than if the company ships directly to customers. That isn't all bad because delivering the product yourself gives you another chance to sell to the customer. But remember to add in a delivery fee to cover your gas or if you have to ship the product to the customer yourself.

 Question

What should I do if I find very little about the company while searching online?
Believe it or not, there are some companies that have almost no online presence, or even an official website, but still would like to convince you that they are a legitimate operation. If all you find is an amateur-looking blog or a website made with a free application, you should move on.

Return policies vary from company to company as well. Some will accept all returns, no questions asked, but many others won't. If the company does not accept returns, this means you will have to negotiate with customers for a solution to their dissatisfaction and may end up reimbursing the full price of the product. If the company does accept returns, find out if you are responsible for filling out any forms and how the customer is reimbursed. These are issues that could affect your workload, especially as your business grows.

Ask People Associated with the Company

Every company has a number of people associated with it. Current and former customers and reps (especially your potential sponsor), vendors, and consultants who have worked with the company can all offer insights about the company you are considering. An ethical company can help you get in touch with some of these people. In fact, a company should be impressed that you are willing to go into this amount of detail in your research, because it shows how committed you are to getting started.

 Essential

Listen closely to people who have decided to part ways with a company. Even stories that sound like sour grapes can tell you a great deal about how a company values people and conducts business on a daily basis. Just be sure to always check facts before passing judgement or making a decision based on people's opinions or experiences.

Utilize social media to ask friends and associates what they know about the company you are researching. A simple question asked on Facebook may draw a litany of answers that you can begin to use in making a judgment.

Checklist: Determining a Solid Company

There are many factors involved in determining whether a company will be the right fit for you. Every company and its representatives will do their utmost to assure you they have your best interests at heart and will provide you with the support you need to succeed. Aside from your own personal considerations, it helps to perform a quick check to be sure the company will stick around in the long term. There are always unpredictable occurrences, such as management takeovers, legal challenges, or a nasty media report that can play a role in a company's future success. You will need to be aware of issues like this and prepare for them.

 Alert

> Companies have definite personalities that don't change quickly. If a company is secretive today, more than likely it will be tomorrow. If employees see your questions as a bother today, they probably will when you're a rep too.

☐ Do the owners and executives have prior experience in the industry? The business of network marketing is unlike most others. The combination of handling product launches, developing new markets, supporting an independent sales force, and working within government guidelines can be difficult at best. Nothing beats past experience in these areas.

☐ Have you checked the reputation and history of the company's owners? As with any industry, some proprietors carry an exemplary record, and some seem to spend more time in the courtroom than the boardroom. Search the company's website to check out who the owners are and then do a brief search to establish whether they are people you are comfortable in partnering with.

☐ Does the compensation plan make sense? Plans can be difficult to understand at first, but you should be able to work out what it takes to earn an income. If you are finding that it takes two or three distributors to explain the plan, you have to consider how difficult it will also be for you to explain it to others.

☐ Is the company's culture one you want to be part of? As you research various companies, it doesn't take long before you get a sense for the community and culture that permeates through the organization. You'll want to be aware of this, as many businesses may have religious, political, or ethical preferences that may not be in line with your own.

☐ Are you comfortable with the company's mission statement? This is usually found on a website's first page or an About Us section. The mission statement will reflect how the company sees itself helping the community and furthering the goals of its distributors.

☐ Does the company provide solid representative support? This includes what happens in customer service, e-mail communication with representatives, and marketing support. A good company understands that happy, profitable, independent business owners build a strong company. Ask other reps about their own experiences and don't be afraid to contact the company directly to ask what support is available.

☐ Are the start-up costs out of range for most prospects? If you will be asking potential team members for more than $2,000 or $3,000 to get started, you may find it difficult to bring in enough people who can afford to make the investment.

CHAPTER 8

Finding a Sponsor

Finding the right sponsor can be a lot like finding the right spouse. Liking the person goes a long way, but the marriage will be stronger if you find someone who is willing to work for your success and complements your weak areas. When you are looking for a sponsor, you want to find a team player who knows how to lead and coach, not someone who sees you as a big dollar sign.

What to Expect from Your Sponsor

Your sponsor is your lifeline to the company. When you first begin working as a rep, you will turn to your sponsor for everything from advice on making a sale to boosting your morale when you have a bad week. Your sponsor will know the people to call at the company when your paperwork is screwed up, your orders don't arrive on time, or you need extra training in a specific area.

 Essential

Your sponsor may sometimes be someone who has been in the business just a few weeks before you joined, so she may also be learning the ropes just like you. If that is the case, you can approach the person above her to get the information you need.

Think of the relationship between you and your sponsor as a team effort. You are not your sponsor's employee or subordinate. You don't have to do exactly what the sponsor says, as if he were your boss, and you can expect the sponsor to share more information with you than many bosses would.

Responsiveness

A good sponsor will be responsive to your needs. You can rely on your sponsor to answer any question you have in a timely manner, even if she works another full-time job, is traveling on business, or is on vacation. Likewise, if you say you're having trouble making cold calls or finding people to talk to, the sponsor should help you find the appropriate training or make some calls with you.

Responsiveness can be proactive as well. Although the sponsor might check in with you every few weeks to see how things are going or notice if your activity has dropped off, the bottom line is that it is *your* business and *your* responsibility to ask your sponsor for help and guidance. Be proactive. For example, if you're having trouble with your product orders, or if all your presentations to potential distributors seem to produce no results, contact your sponsor. In these situations—and many more—the sponsor can give personal advice or recommend training materials long before you have to ask for it.

 Question

What if my sponsor and I don't get along?
You don't have to work directly with your sponsor if you feel there is a mismatch. Find someone upline you can work with and continue to grow your business.

Respect

You should trust your sponsor to respect you, treat you as a professional, and guide you into new areas. The sponsor shouldn't make you feel dumb, no matter how basic your questions may be, and has no right to be patronizing.

Respect comes in many forms. First, your sponsor should respect your reasons for getting into network marketing. For example, if you never intend to pursue this as a full-time career, the sponsor shouldn't try to convince you to change your mind. Likewise, if you prefer to sell products and not concentrate too much on attracting additional distributors into your downline, that also is a decision your sponsor should respect.

 Alert

Respect is the most important ingredient in your relationship with your sponsor. If your sponsor doesn't respect you, he will be unable to provide you with the advice and environment you need to succeed.

The sponsor should also respect the way you do business. Hopefully, your sponsor has had a fair amount of success in her network marketing business, and you should learn from that success, but that doesn't mean you have to do everything exactly the same way she did. If you prefer a soft sell over a hard sell, the choice should be left up to you.

Mentoring Ability

The best sponsors are not just good at network marketing; they know how to teach other people to be good at it too. Chances are, you have met many people in your life who were excellent at something—sewing, hunting, dog training, swimming, public speaking—but could never teach their skills to anybody. The fact is, things come so naturally to some people that they just can't explain how to do it.

If that's the case with your potential sponsor, ask her quite candidly if there is someone further upline who could help you. There is nothing more frustrating than someone who says, "Just do it!" when you mention that you're having trouble in a specific area. Instead, you want someone who can patiently take you through every step of the process. You want someone who remembers exactly how she did something and can tell you just how to do it.

A good mentor has the ability to give you the right information even before you need it. She tells you what the next step will be and what her personal plans are for the business. If she hears about a new product line coming out, that information should be passed on to you as soon as possible if she is in a position to divulge that.

 Fact

A good mentor is both a friend and an advisor. She will tell you when you are doing something wrong and suggest a solution. She also will praise you when you do something right.

The best mentors know how to give a gentle push and some encouragement toward success. Your sponsor should constantly tell you that she knows you can do better because you have it in you.

A good mentor also knows how to motivate you. If you're having a bad week, the mentor knows if you need a pep talk, a new goal, a "me too" chat, or some additional training. She should know whether you like difficult goals or find them too intimidating, whether you like to be praised in public or find it embarrassing, and whether you can take honest criticism well or whether it needs to be softened a bit.

A True Relationship

You should feel quite comfortable in letting your hair down every now and then and socialize with your sponsor. This business is not all about having your nose to the grindstone attending events, sponsoring new people, and having a phone glued to your ear. The saying that you should never mix business with pleasure doesn't necessarily ring true in network marketing. You'll often be spending time with your sponsor having dinners with your team, traveling to different locations, or organizing an end-of-year Christmas party for your organization.

Friendship Isn't Always the Best Policy

Good friends and family members may not always be the best sponsors, simply because they like you and know you too well. They might have difficulty telling you the truth because they are afraid of the repercussions. Could your younger brother really tell you that you need some heavy-duty sales training or that you don't understand the product well enough yet?

 Essential

Some companies allow "sponsor shopping," where experienced distributors will decide which company they want to partner with and then interview prospective sponsors to discover the best fit for their personality and goals.

Friends and family might trust you too much. They may assume that because you are a friend or relative, you will work hard for them no matter what. As a result, they won't work to motivate you, and they might give you far less attention than they would someone else.

Of course, there are exceptions to every rule. There are some friends and family members who make excellent sponsors. The key is to examine your reasons carefully and be honest with yourself. If your friend or relative is a true business leader who will respect you as a person and let you run the business the way you want, you could end up having a great working relationship. Not only will you be getting the support you need, but every sale you make will be helping a good friend or family member too.

Look at the Track Record

The best predictor of a person's value as a sponsor is how well she does with her own network marketing business. You will want to examine everything from how long it took your sponsor to build a good downline to how much product she personally uses every month.

Don't be shy when you ask about your sponsor's track record. Unless you are a natural networker, you will be modeling many of your strategies and tactics on her success. It's important that your sponsor is either reasonably successful or working with someone that is, and understands and can educate you on the reasons behind that success.

 Fact

A good sponsor will have a well-balanced business resume. You want to see just enough failure to know the person can empathize with you and has had an opportunity to learn from his mistakes. Too much early success can make a person cocky and unsympathetic.

At the same time, a good track record is not enough. Remember that you are entering the business at a different point. Your sponsor may have been successful in the past—when the product line was still unique and before the competition really took off. Would the sponsor have been as successful in the current market?

Your Sponsor's Downline

Before you choose a sponsor, take the time to speak with members of his team. Ideally, the sponsor should already be working with at least three or four other people. However, everyone has to start somewhere, so you could end up being the first in someone's downline. Although that situation can be riskier than entering a thriving organization, it can also be exciting because you can work as a team to build the business.

Assuming there are others in the downline, ask to talk to two or three of them. Are they happy? What does the sponsor do to support them? Would they like more support? Is the motivation good? Do they feel pushed and cajoled, or do they feel they are given adequate respect when trying to reach a goal? Does the sponsor communicate his expectations?

Failures Are Okay

When Lee Iacocca was hired by Chrysler in 1978 to turn around the company's business, the board of directors was impressed that he had been in charge of the failed Edsel division. Why? Because they reasoned that since he had made his share of mistakes, he would also know how to avoid them.

You want a sponsor who has seen a bit of adversity in his business. If everything has been great for the sponsor, he won't be able to relate to your problems and will expect you to do just as well as he did.

Success Counts

While a bit of failure is good for any businessperson due to the lessons learned, you also want to see success. You want to be assured that this person knows how to succeed in network marketing so that she can pass those skills on to you. You have to believe with all your being that this person is the one that will help you to be successful.

In terms of recruiting new distributors, look for someone who has not only shown they are able to recruit effectively, but whose downline has stayed in business. That means your sponsor understands how to sell the business to others, as well as how to keep a downline motivated.

In terms of selling the product, look for someone who makes at least 10 percent of her income from direct sales. You want to make sure that this person is staying with the business, believes in the product, and has experience meeting new sales challenges as they arise.

Ask the Right Questions

Some network marketers are excellent at developing an invitation you can't say no to. They lay out everything so perfectly and it all sounds so wonderful that you're ready to sign the application and hand over your credit card before the presentation has even ended.

If that urge strikes you, it's time to step back and suggest a formal interview with the prospective sponsor, even if he is a good friend or family member. You want to make sure that the person is sincere about helping you succeed, not just when he is making a formal presentation to you.

Suggest a neutral spot such as a local restaurant or Starbucks so that you can ask questions without the pressures of a formal presentation. Bring a notebook and write one of the following questions at the top of each page. Also add any additional questions you might have about the products or the company. Don't leave the table until you have an answer to every question!

Why Do You Want Me to Join?

If your sponsor wants you as part of his downline in order to get a bonus or make more money, that's okay, but it may make you question his motives. He should sincerely believe that he is inviting you to an opportunity that will enhance your life and that you can do very well in. Avoid sponsors who seem to spout marketing talk such as "This is the opportunity of a lifetime" or "You'd be crazy not to do this." The choice you make should be made on genuine facts and rational reasons, not hype and inflated claims.

 Essential

Continue to ask questions until you get to the heart of the prospective sponsor. Don't accept prepared answers. Look for someone who thinks carefully before responding to your questions.

How Much Do You Want to Grow in This Business?

A good answer is that the person views this as a job and knows there is room for growth. Be wary of people who say they want to become millionaires and then retire (and live off your hard work).

Look for realistic expectations here. If you have done your research on the product and have found that it has a relatively small niche in the marketplace, be wary of someone who says he wants all his team members to have 100 customers in their first twelve months.

How Much Work Will I Need to Put In?

If your sponsor starts talking about full-time work and the wonderful income potential, and you're not yet ready for that leap, ask exactly how you can work the business part-time and still achieve your goals. You want someone who is flexible enough to understand that you might not want to jump in full-time right away.

What's Your Mission?

Good sponsors will have missions that go beyond money. Sure, they may want to become millionaires and retire early, but they should also say that they like to be self-employed, that they like to work with people, that they believe in this product, and that when it comes to being a sponsor, they want to help their people reach their goals and fulfill their potential.

 Alert

Ask enough questions to determine what motivates your potential sponsor. Even if you have nothing in common with your sponsor, you will have a better sense of how this person judges success and what she wants out of life.

How Can You Help Me Succeed?

Many prospective sponsors will be taken aback by this question. In response, they might mention all the support the company offers and may make vague references to their experience. While these people aren't necessarily bad sponsors, there are others who could do better.

If you find a prospective sponsor who responds by saying that he will spend at least one day a month with you for the first three months helping you learn the products and the company while also helping you make sales calls, you know you've found a very good sponsor.

Similarly, if a prospective sponsor tells you that he personally produces a one-page newsletter that reviews successes people have had with difficult customers or entering new markets and distributes this newsletter to his downline, you are in good shape. Many good sponsors will also talk about meetings they hold for everyone in their downline and how they encourage the sharing of sales strategies among their downline.

How Do You Communicate with Your Team?

Communication is a key component in any business relationship. As a downline member, you want to know what is going on with your sponsor. Has she recruited any new distributors? Has there been an increase in sales? Is there any more information that can be passed along? Are there any sales secrets to be shared?

You also need to know what is happening at the company. While the company will most likely communicate directly with you on major issues, your sponsor has been around longer than you and may be plugged into events you aren't aware of.

Be sure to find out how your sponsor prefers to communicate with his team. Some may prefer e-mail or text messages, while others will call you to relay a message. You'll want to make it clear how you prefer to be communicated with and when.

The Sponsor's Sponsor

Remember that you are not just signing up to be a member of your sponsor's downline. You are part of the downline of everyone above your sponsor as well. Much of the support you get will be modeled on the support your own sponsor receives from her upline. You should be invited to meetings sponsored by your upline and receive written communications they offer. Likewise, if you have any questions about the business, you should be free to call these people for help.

Your sponsor's sponsor is especially important if your prospective sponsor is relatively new in the business. If you are one of his first recruits, you want to know that you will be taken care of by someone with a little more experience. In fact, you may want to interview this person as closely as you do the prospective sponsor.

Even more important, these people can help you determine if your prospective sponsor is a good fit for you. Ask about your prospective sponsor's communication style. Find out what your prospective sponsor's strengths and weaknesses are.

 Essential

Your sponsor's sponsor is the best indicator of the type of support you will receive from your own sponsor. Look for someone higher up who is still involved in the business and offers good advice to your sponsor without being too controlling.

No matter what your final decision is regarding a sponsor, remember that you have many people in your upline to help you. Be sure they are willing to help; then use them wisely.

CHAPTER 9

Starting Your Business

Learning all about the industry is one thing, but getting involved in it is when things become exciting. Once you have chosen your company and a product line, it's time to launch your business and begin to grow your organization. The great part is it can be a short learning curve, and help is available through many resources. You just have to decide what you want out of the business, and be prepared to roll up your sleeves and get to work.

Set Yourself Up for Success

You've signed your application form, submitted it online, and are now registered as a new rep. You're excited about your new business and the future that lays ahead. While you have a fair understanding of what it's going to take to make the business work, you also know not everyone succeeds in network marketing, and you don't want to become another statistic.

The very first thing you should do is get a feel for how the back office works. This will be an online portal, usually accessible through your company's home page, which allows you to provide your personal details, track and make orders, and see how your organization is developing. There may be a small cost of $20–$50 per month to access this service, or it could be free, but either way, accessing this tool is necessary for your business. It will be extremely difficult to build a business without access to your virtual office. Spend some time looking at what information it offers you, and be sure you add in important details like the credit card you would prefer to use when ordering product, the bank account you would like your commissions paid to, and the address of where the products must be delivered and the customers and consultants you have in your downline.

 Essential

A back office is an online tool provided by your company to view your sales volume, organization, new team members, and to make product orders. It is vital that you have one to be able to build your business.

If your company has an autoship service, this is where you can adjust which products you order and set which day you want the delivery, if your company allows for options in that area. Check with your sponsor to see when the next major event is on in your area. There may not be one for several weeks, or there may be one in another city that you are encouraged to attend. Whether you go or not will be based on your commitment level, but ideally you should do what you can to be there. Make this decision to attend the very next event as soon as you sign up.

Your starter kit will usually include a basic welcome package, a message from the CEO, product information, and a basic training booklet. These are often called "Roadmap to Success" or "Your Business Plan" or something similar. It is imperative you take the time go through this manual, as it is put together by leaders in your company who are experienced in building a business.

Next you'll need to find a place in your home where you can conduct your business. This doesn't have to be fancy or spacious. As long as you have access to a phone, a computer with Internet, and a printer, you are set to go. Some basic stationery will be needed, but don't go overboard with buying anything that is not crucial in the early stages. If your company offers business cards and personalized stationery, look into getting hold of some, as that will help brand what you do and create a good impression with those you prospect.

 Alert

As you set up your business, don't get stuck into getting ready to get ready. It's easy to procrastinate by creating complicated filing systems and reading and re-reading your starter guide. Those things are needed, but they don't make you money and they don't grow your team.

Vital Tools You Need

Network marketing has become such a portable business that the actual tools required to operate your business are now easily transported almost anywhere you are around the world. As long as you have access to a smartphone with Internet access, you can basically run your business. Phone applications such as WhatsApp, Periscope, and Viber now give you the opportunity to stay in touch with your prospects and team members, keeping them updated with where you are and what they need to know. A reliable laptop, or a tablet like a Samsung Galaxy or iPad, is now all you require in terms of technology to help stay on top of your business.

You will, however, need to look at tools and resources available from your company that will help you professionally promote your business and products. These include catalogs, company information on DVD or CD, pamphlets that offer product information, success-story CDs, and online audio or magazines designed to share success stories with your customers and prospective team members. The most prominent and widely recognized magazine used among network marketers is *Success from Home*, from the publishers of *Success* magazine. Each year, twelve direct-selling companies are chosen to be featured, and each issue is available for one month at bookstores such as Barnes & Noble.

 Alert

> Avoid the temptation to load up your shelves with every tool available without being determined to use them. A tool only works when you give it to a prospect or team member; tools won't do a thing gathering dust on your shelf at home.

Check with your sponsor and determine which tools your team is using. Go through each one to get an idea of what is most effective. Some tools may work well for some reps but may not be something you feel comfortable using.

At minimum, you should always keep on hand material that explains how the business works, what range of products your company offers and why they are needed, and either a video or paper presentation of your compensation plan.

Managing Your Time

The secret to success in any business endeavor is using your time wisely. You don't have to be a sales wizard or a business genius to succeed in network marketing as long as you keep working at it productively. Organize yourself, lose those time-wasting habits, and replace them with new, more productive ones.

Managing your time can be one of the most difficult aspects of building your business. Most people building a network marketing business are already busy. They have work commitments, families to attend to, weekend sports, and a few minutes here and there to relax and wind down.

If you can carve out just five to fifteen hours a week, part-time and spread over the seven days to build your business, you can achieve the success you are looking for. That's just forty minutes a day at least to commit to making your prospecting calls and follow-ups.

 Essential

Perhaps one of the most important advantages of network marketing is its flexibility. You're not stuck behind a desk or an office cubicle. As long as you have access to a phone and the Internet, you can practically run your business from anywhere in the world.

Every now and then you will need to attend a local event, but you will even then only increase your time commitment by a manageable period. Top earner and the author of *Beach Money*, Jordan Adler, famously built his business doing all his prospecting meetings and follow-ups during his short lunch breaks at work. Debbie Atkinson built her multimillion-dollar business working as a nurse and making calls on her fifteen-minute breaks.

You will need to be disciplined in how you allocate and use your time. Let your family know that at certain times of the day you will need to be on the phone with no interruptions. You'll need to set aside time for prospecting calls, follow-up calls, calls to team members and customers, and attending events and any webinars or conference calls your company or team holds. Some of these activities can be performed via e-mail, text messaging, or chat apps like Facebook Messenger. Whatever you can do to be as efficient as possible in using your time will go a long way toward the success of your business.

How Much Will It Cost?

Alongside your initial starter kit, you will need to allocate a part of your budget to ongoing business costs and product purchases. Every business has some form of overhead and expenses, and network marketing is no different. The good news is that these expenses are relatively affordable for most reps to begin with. Most costs are broken down into the following categories:

Monthly or Weekly Orders

Almost every company will require you to make some sort of product or service order for you to stay commission qualified. This order may be for your own personal use or to sell to a retail customer. This is a vital part of your business, as it also means you will be able to experience results with the products and create a testimonial. You will most likely be able to use autoship, an automatic shipment of products, to fulfill this objective without having to remember to place an order every month. Autoship amounts vary from company to company, but you should budget around $150–$200 to cover this product cost.

Communication Costs

You will be spending a lot of time on the phone and Internet, staying in touch with prospects, your team, and the company. As costs with communication companies vary so greatly, it isn't possible to estimate what you will be paying for these services.

If you are finding it difficult to keep your phone costs down, take a look at free apps such as WhatsApp, Viber, and Tango. Skype has been a favorite for networkers for several years now, and is an excellent tool to use when delivering a short presentation to your prospect. Facebook allows you to call friends directly from its smartphone app. Just look for the Call icon on your Facebook friends' personal Page, and as long as you have Internet access, they will receive your direct call.

Tools and Resources

You will need some company tools in order to promote your business. Prospecting DVDs, product information, magazines, compensation plan descriptions, and sponsoring websites are all tools you should be taking advantage of. Professional tools are a much better and more effective option than creating your own or making poor copies. Invest in professional tools and get them into the hands of genuinely interested prospects. Remember, marketing tools are an investment that can bring you many, many times their cost.

Travel Expenses

Travel may not be so much of an issue in your early days, but as your team expands you may be expected to get on a plane or drive to a city three or four hours away to help support team members and drum up new business. Many company events may also be held in another city or state. Your company's convention may also be held in another country. In Asia, reps from many countries such as Thailand, Malaysia, and Singapore will often travel to Hong Kong or Indonesia to attend conventions. Also keep in mind that gas in your tank and general vehicle maintenance will come into play if you are doing a lot of driving around to deliver product or meet new prospects.

These are the most common types of expenses that pop up in your network marketing business, but you should also expect to occasionally pay for coffee, tea, and even meals when meeting with your team and prospects. Just remember to keep receipts and records for all your expenditures. If you are running your business properly, many of these expenses could be tax deductible. Be sure to check with your accountant to clarify your position and what you can and cannot claim.

What to Expect from the Company

Your company essentially has two main roles. The first is to provide a high-quality product or service that offers good value for money and provides you with a needed result. The second is to pay you, at agreed times and for agreed sales volumes, a commission and other rewards in the compensation plan when they are deemed due.

There are different thoughts as to whether companies should or need to get involved with marketing by providing tools or setting up events. Some leaders see this as the role of the reps, who should be free to construct all forms of marketing and training to suit the way they want to build their teams and shape organizational culture, as long as it falls within the boundaries set by the company. Others argue that the company should be responsible for almost everything in this area, and that anything produced by reps should be taken as a bonus. There are companies using, and succeeding, with both philosophies. But a middle ground has been reached in most, where a combination of both company-produced and leader-produced resources are available to the reps.

 Essential

A strong network marketing company can offer many resources for you to use. And unlike franchise owners, you will be free to pick and choose the resources that best meet your needs.

What you will most often see is that smaller training meetings are being led by leaders of different organizations, while larger conventions and rallies are staged by the corporate office, taking into account the larger costs associated with these events. Tools and marketing resources, including websites and printed material, are the domain of the company in order for the company to send out a consistent, uniform message with every format.

There is one area that every company should take the lead: distributor services. Your company should have a dedicated division that handles everything from product returns to new representative applications, with online links to common questions. Ideally, this service should be easy to contact in various ways including via social media channels, e-mail, phone, and real-time chat directly from the company's site.

Creating a Home Office

Virtually all network marketing opportunities are designed to be operated out of a home office, saving you a great deal of money in start-up expenses as compared to any other type of business opportunity, whether a franchise operation or a conventional business.

There's no need to start with an expensive outlay on your home office. A smartphone, reasonably new computer, and a printer is more than enough to get you started. You will also need pens on hand and paper to print on. It may also help to have a whiteboard that you can use in keeping major ideas constantly in front of you.

 Essential

If you are planning to purchase a desk for your workspace, think small. Large desks are just a place to store clutter that can get lost and distract you. A smaller desk encourages you to get the work done because the papers keep getting in your way!

The key to making a home office work is to have a dedicated area where everyone in your family knows you work at specific times. If you use your kitchen table for a desk, that's fine as long as the family knows that it's off-limits to them during your work hours. Likewise, you can use a corner of the living room, your bedroom, or any other space as long as everyone knows that this is your office. Many reps have turned sections of their garage into their home office, as it often means they can work at home but away from the main area where the family is located. If you can close a door, that's wonderful. If not, some people buy portable screens that mark off their workspace.

 Fact

> Your family and friends will respect your work time as long as they see you working. Don't let them disturb you, and they will soon come to understand that this is as much of a job as if you commuted to an office every day.

Don't fret too much about setting up elaborate filing systems to house company information and prospect details. We live in times where all of this can sit inside your PC or Mac, or even an iPad. Microsoft's Office software will provide you with every type of resource needed in order to manage your communications and keep electronic files. E-mail programs are abundant on the Internet, with Gmail from Google, Yahoo! Mail, and Microsoft's free version of Outlook being the most prominent.

The last thing you should consider is a small bookshelf where you can keep recruiting tools and company information located. This will make them easier to find when you need to send them out, and help you stay aware of anything that may be running out and needs to be re-ordered.

CHAPTER 10

Learning Basic Sales Skills

Network marketing is not your typical sales business. While some people may view selling as an uncomfortable, often awkward process, and one that they could never embrace, even the most introverted, sales-averse individuals have experienced incredible success in this industry. A focus on team support, recognition, and a softer approach to recommending valued products and services has helped many reps create significant incomes.

Working with Sales Scripts

You may initially be uncomfortable with the idea of working with a script, but over time you will find that being aware of what you are going to say before you have to say it is a valuable attribute that you will make use of many times over. Look to your upline and company training material for scripts related to inviting, making follow-up calls, and answering objections related to both the business and the product.

 Alert

Perhaps your company has offered you sales training and helped you come up with a sales script. If not, you will want to create one for yourself. It will come in very handy when it's time for you talk about your business.

Once you have settled on a script you can see yourself using, it's important that you practice it over and over again until you can say the words without reading them and do it fluently and without hesitation. One successful network marketer would read his scripts to his attentive basset hound over and over again until he felt that not only was he reciting them flawlessly, but the dog could as well!

Developing a Powerful Invitation

A good invitation can be the key to getting new prospects to look at your business. That's because your invitation will play a big part in whether somebody will choose to look at what you have to share or take a pass. A weak invitation can have you running in circles wondering why nobody is interested in viewing your presentation. And a good one could mean you have a whole week lined up with prospects eager to hear what you have to say.

As with all scripts, it's important you sit down with your sponsor and go through company training that will educate you on what to say and when to say it. The invitation is such an important part of starting and growing your business that almost every starter kit and first training session will include a whole section on this key element.

 Alert

Older companies would often try to hide the name of the company during the initial invitation, an approach that isn't practical in today's market. Prospects want to know upfront which company you are with and what the product is, and they need a convincing reason why they should view your presentation.

When you make your invitation, be sure not to come across as overbearing or aggressive. You also don't want to appear needy, coming off as though you are desperate for your prospect to check out your product line or opportunity. People don't respond in a positive way when they feel you need them more than they need you, particularly when it comes to looking at business opportunities or something to buy.

As much as possible, try to make every invitation over the phone, a strategy that is used by almost every top income earner in the industry. The reasoning is that you can then keep the conversation short and to the point, and can end the call rapidly if your prospect wants to tell you the stories of how her aunt Norma knew a guy who married his cousin and had two children that never did much with "one of those things." If you are making invitations face-to-face, then you are going to hear a lot of those stories. On a long-haul flight, that could mean begging to move seats or a desperate search for a parachute.

Selling Your Opportunity and Selling Your Products

Your prospects are looking for solutions to their problems. Sally wants to find a way to control her utility bills, which have burned a hole in her budget since she had the twins. If someone could show her a better, lower-priced, and reliable option, she is ready to sign. Konrad is tired of spending Monday mornings fighting traffic, rushing into 7 A.M. meetings chaired by an ungrateful manager. He would much prefer to work from home and sleep in. But what options are out there? Norman is concerned with the weight he has gained since he stopped playing sports. He wants to control his weight, but the weight-loss tablets he used in the past were difficult to swallow and gave him stomach pains. He would much prefer a delicious shake, but where can he find one that agrees with his sensitive digestive system?

These are just some of the everyday challenges your prospects are facing, and they are desperate for solutions.

By digging for clues with some well-thought-out questions, your prospects will open up and reveal to you all you need to know about exactly what their issues are and how you can sell them on the answers. For some people, that may mean focusing on the benefits of your products and how the products can potentially help them overcome pressing health challenges. Others will be searching for an opportunity to supplement their income or even finding avenues to get away from the eight-to-faint grind and develop a more satisfactory lifestyle working from home.

But how do you discover what you should lead with and what will most likely appeal to your target market? People should obviously want both, right?

Not quite.

The idea of building a part-time home business is attractive to some people, while your products' benefits will appeal more to others. If Billy asks you for a solution to his gout problem and you then invite him to your business presentation at the Holiday Inn, you've probably lost him as a customer. If Mariam reveals she's looking for a side business selling homewares, and you offer to sell her your hip apron line, but neglect to tell her how she can make money selling them too, you may end up losing your next top consultant.

Leading with your products will help you create a lot of product awareness and create many great testimonials, but basically becoming a product salesman could mean you are living principally on the retail profits. You will also need to provide your customers with regular product updates, share other testimonials, and suggest products in your range that could complement what they are currently buying from you. Also, keep in mind that retail and preferred customers won't always recommend what they are using to others, particularly as there is no financial incentive to do so. Yes, their results in using what you sell them may be noticed—particularly ones that revolve around weight loss and beauty care—but they will more often simply be happy in using a product that is good value for their money, convenient to purchase, and accomplishes what they have bought it for.

Leading with the business, however, means you can attract reps who will both use the products and recruit other reps. With every new recruit that comes into the fold, the opportunity to grow market share, increase your group's sales volume, and strengthen your organization increases.

Some people will never have an interest in your product line or business, others will like the business idea but can't get enthusiastic about your product line, and some will ask, "Where have you been all of my life?" They are the ones who will get involved in your business, create a whirlwind of excitement in your group, and inspire others to succeed with your opportunity.

It would be nice if there was a way to predict who is going to go where, but marketing would simply not exist if life was that predictable. It will be your job to peel away the layers of every prospect to determine where he stands and what he is looking for. This is where good listening skills become invaluable, and empathy with your prospects will be greatly valued. They don't want to be forced into doing anything. They want to make a choice that suits them, and when they make that choice, they want to be certain that they have your support no matter their decision.

Handling Common Objections

Objections are a natural part of the selling and buying process. It can often feel like your prospects will create an objection only so they don't appear to be too eager to make a purchase without doing any research. Being perceived as an easy target causes many men and women to become defensive, which leads them to offer common and predictable objections to help stall the sales process while they consider matters that often have no relation to their verbal objection.

In some cases, people like to throw up objections just to see if you can stay professional while they make your life difficult. In other cases, people have real reservations that you have to help them overcome.

 Essential

Objections are a fact of life in the sales world. Don't take them too seriously or feel as though you have failed if you can't overcome every objection thrown at you. Some objections are just meant to be a polite way of saying no.

Be careful when dealing with objections, though. Sometimes people just want to say something to make you go away. For some reason you haven't discovered the need that will make them buy your product. Or maybe your business truly isn't a good fit for them. Whatever the reason, if they continue to object after you have resolved the first few objections, you are better off leaving for the moment. You can always give them a call in a few weeks or even months down the track.

Here are some simple ways to overcome common objections in network marketing:

- *"The product costs too much."* Compare it to the cost per dose. Also compare it to products of similar quality.
- *"I don't buy anything I can't see."* Offer to take the product back if they don't like it, or remind them of any guarantees your company offers.
- *"I already have enough of that kind of stuff."* Point out how this is better than what they currently use, and back that up with third-party research if possible.
- *"I don't have the money."* Ask them when they want to stop being in that position. Let them know that many people

join your business that have been in similar financial situations, but through diligent effort and a desire to improve their life, they are now financially free.

- *"I never buy from door-to-door salespeople."* Explain that you don't sell door-to-door; you sell directly to customers. You don't knock on any doors unless you know the people are interested and you have been invited to see them.
- *"I don't have the time."* Provide a list of what they can achieve if they give the business just one hour a day and learn to leverage their time.
- *"I'm just not a salesperson."* They don't need to be. Your company will provide tools and educational resources that your prospect will evaluate and be able to make her own decision as to whether she wants your products or be involved in the business.
- *"I think network marketing is a scam."* Business icons such as Warren Buffett, Donald Trump, and financial author Robert Kiyosaki have all endorsed the industry. Would they all put their name unwittingly to an illegal scam?
- *"I'm shy."* Many of the biggest success stories in the industry are naturally shy, introverted people. In fact, being shy could be an asset, as people often feel more comfortable around those who are calm and collected.
- *"I'd like to, but my spouse would be angry."* It's normal to have your spouse question your purchases and business decisions. Just know that when your commissions start to come in or you earn something exotic like a free trip to Maui, your spouse will become extremely supportive in record time.
- *"I'm not smart enough; it's too complicated."* Remind them of all the training and support materials, events, and upline support that is available.

Selling Without Being Pushy

One of the most unpleasant criticisms that any salesman or marketer can hear is that he or she is "pushy." The term is used to describe a salesman who will essentially make light of all questions from the prospect and downplay any objections. His only goal is to make a sale at any cost. Not only do consumers greatly dislike this type of consultant, but they go out of their way to avoid them.

Other salespeople, witnessing their colleagues behave so unprofessionally, decide that being pushy is something they never want to be seen as doing. They want to be liked by the prospect, and don't want to do anything that can make them appear too desperate to make the sale. A hard, pushy close is viewed as the hallmark of an amateur or someone keen to sell and disappear fast.

Network marketers are also highly conscious of the customer reaction in this situation and are just as keen to not be stricken with Pushy Salesman Syndrome. Remember: people will buy from you when they know you, like you, and trust you. If you start with all three before your presentation, you're already halfway across the line.

 Essential

Listening doesn't necessarily mean being silent while the other person talks. It means actively listening to the other person's problems and concerns; it means asking questions and knowing what clues signal a true need. Good listeners don't try to get ahead of the discussion.

If you are meeting with someone for the first time or following up to get an answer, you would do well to keep in mind that the network marketing business is a voluntary one. You can't force people into becoming reps just as you can't force them to buy your product. They will make a positive decision once they have confirmed in their mind that they see value in the product, need it, and can afford it. Cover those three requisites and you basically have a sale.

A good network marketer, through asking questions and intently listening to the answers, will form a trust with the prospect that will lead to the prospect's respecting your opinion. Your listening and understanding has to be genuine, and your prospect will sense if it is not.

When you get a sense that you have built good rapport, you can then get into how you can help your prospect based on what she wants and what your business or product can do. This process will essentially avoid your having to resort to a pushy sale, since your prospect has already been open about what it is she wants and you are simply offering the solution. Your attitude now is that it is her decision as to whether she takes advantage of it or not. Either way, your job is to present her with the solution, not to ram it down her throat!

If you talk her into the business, you'll be talking her into doing the business. You'll be on the phone constantly reminding her about every meeting, every webinar, and about placing a product order.

When people join you and it is their own choice, this type of harassment is never needed. But when pushy network marketers bring people into the business that really don't want to be there, they are doomed to a career of filling a leaky bucket where they are unwittingly drilling the holes.

Understanding the Mind of the Consumer

The marketplace is extraordinarily cluttered. People have lots of choices to make about what to buy and from whom. Most people will tell you that they have too many choices and are bombarded with too many messages that try to convince them that one product really is better than another. Just look at the toothpaste aisle in your grocery store. Yes, every product is slightly different. It may be a different color, or have a different taste, or parade some other little distinguishing characteristic. But is there one product that's inarguably the best? Not likely.

This trend began in the postwar production era of the 1950s. For generations who had primarily been raised in rural areas, the sudden access to "stuff" was very exciting. Large department stores and shopping malls were designed to provide a smorgasbord of products to eager customers. While this has provided the consumer with a vast selection to choose from, it has also created confusion for those who are unsure of what is the best option and why.

Consumer advocates and fringe groups representing everything from banning cow meat to regulating working conditions in the Philippines have helped inform a public that scrutinizes what it buys and where the money goes. The next cell phone you choose to buy will either help pay for a family's new car in Vietnam or drive your next-door neighbor out of his job. Such are the quirks of today's global economy.

Emerging from this uncertainty and confusion is a consumer unsure of who to trust and what to listen for. Today's consumers, desiring a sense of certainty and trust, are turning to their friends and family to recommend everything from hair care, nutritional supplements, and laundry soap to scented candles, essential oils, and cell phones. The power of word-of-mouth referral is stronger than ever, with a consumer market open to its benefits and an industry primed to be at the forefront of the next economic wave.

Building a Customer Base

Whether you are focused on building a large organization of representatives and customers or simply want to earn a few hundred dollars in retail profits, it is important that you develop a base of customers that happily use your product. This can be formed from your friends and family who are happy to support your business, as well as people you come across who may signal a need for what you are marketing.

 Fact

One organization in Italy created a system where the first order for new team members was slightly double the conventional amount. They then supported and trained the new reps to invite everyone they knew to check out the new line of products they were marketing.

An upline was on hand during the night, explaining the product's benefits and features and helping create a successful night of retail sales for the new team members. Not only did the team members earn a handsome profit on the night, but they were taking requests weeks later for more product from satisfied customers.

Your upline will have many ideas to help create your customer base that may revolve around having similar product nights or handing out samples and organizing an afternoon skin-care party. It is one part of your business where the potential to create profit through sales and long-term income through volume growth are truly endless.

CHAPTER 11

The Financially Free Mindset

M ost network marketers have a goal of being "financially free." It doesn't really matter how much money you make; becoming financially free is having enough money coming in every month to pay all your bills and not working for it. This is really the premise of network marketing—to build residual income on a monthly basis. But you must develop the mindset and vision to do so. While developing your skills and learning strategies and scripts play a significant role in your business, being persistent, being positive, and having the desire to succeed are the character traits that will help shape your success.

The Power of Personal Development

Personal development is a process you undertake, utilizing multiple resources, to help develop your thinking and skills in order to achieve a higher level in your life. It's not just about improvement in your business life. Many people immerse themselves in personal development to develop better relationships, create greater self-confidence, or overcome a perceived character weakness.

Your daily experiences shape your attitude and your behavior:

- You can't watch the nightly news without it affecting the way you think.
- You can't attend your company convention without your belief level soaring.

- You can't read an inspiring story in the morning and not have it impact your day.
- Everything you experience through your senses leaves a mark on your emotional state that either carries you forward or pulls you back.

While you are no doubt getting a daily dose of negative news that would bring anyone down, you can make the choice to fight back. You don't have to be overwhelmed by stories that only make you see the worst in people. There are so many options today to help you become a better person. You can listen to a positive seminar online, read a book, watch a DVD, or attend a two-day retreat in the mountains. There is a multitude of opportunities available for anybody that has chosen to embark on a journey of self-improvement.

Network marketers from every walk of life have utilized personal development to help overcome their initial fears and build confidence in their ability to grow a business. Interestingly, many reps who walk away from the industry often tell how, despite not achieving the financial success they first sought, the high level of personal development and improvement in their people skills played a prominent role in other areas for their lives.

 Essential

Don't expect everyone to understand your personal-development journey. Friends and family can often feel threatened when you decide to make sudden changes. Just be patient and understanding of their view. When the new you emerges, they will privately be very proud.

Whether it's a reading a positive book, listening to a CD, or even sitting in on an uplifting seminar, it's important for you to take at least thirty minutes every day to work on your mindset. Work on understanding people better and becoming a better communicator. Work on your relationships and developing your skills in leading people. It's often been said that your income can only grow to the level that you do. This is why you will so often find in this industry that those that reach the higher levels of success also happen to be reps who started just like everybody else but who put hours and hours into developing themselves first before the money even began to roll in.

You don't want to be someone who learns but refuses to apply the lessons. It's vital you begin to live out what you're reading. Let it show in your daily life. What will make or break you in the next five years of your life is quite simply the people you will meet and choose to listen to. So be sure you are working on that every day. Remember, it doesn't matter what you read, or hear, it only matters what actions you implement.

Personal development is not just for network marketers and people involved in sales. The benefits will show in every area of your life, and you'll be glad that you began your own journey into being a better you.

Discipline and Determination

While discipline is a character trait that many people find hard to implement, you must develop it if you want to succeed in network marketing. If you're prone to procrastination and often put everything aside until later, you'll need to overcome that aspect of your personality and find a way to do what needs to be done. You can only avoid making prospecting and follow-up calls, attending events, and getting on your weekly training webinar for so long. Eventually the lack of discipline is going to leave you struggling to grow a team and allow negativity to set it.

Next is determination—a major character trait you will need to develop when times get tough and things aren't going your way. A good network marketer never gives up. She understands that there are good times and bad times in every business and recognizes the importance of working through the bad times. Ask yourself what you have done in your personal and work life when times got tough. Did you quit your job when the boss started asking too much from you? Did you divorce your spouse when you started having arguments every night? Did you throw your hands in the air and give up when your teenagers caused problems? If that's the case, you might not have the perseverance it takes to make it in this business.

Determination means that the goals you have set for yourself are more important than the obstacles. It means that you will develop the resilience necessary to plough through any setbacks that could set you off your path. This may require you to spend time with your leaders, your sponsor, and even your corporate team so you can get your belief back and get back on track. Whatever it takes, you must stay determined in reaching the goals you have set yourself!

Overcoming Fear

First, it's important that you understand that every person who starts out in this business has fears. In fact, anybody starting any new endeavor has fears. It's totally natural, and it is expected.

It could be a fear of showing the people you know your business or product, in case they may judge your decision. Many reps have a fear of prospecting because they hate facing rejection. For you it may be about speaking in public or getting on a plane to travel to an out-of-country event.

Believe it or not, another common fear is the fear of success. People begin to fret over the responsibilities that may crop up when they become leaders in the business. They imagine being hounded to loan out money, or having to speak on stage at a major event and end up doing a terrible job.

Some people fear being "found out" when they achieve success. This is actually more frequent than you think. They think that when they reach a high level of achievement somebody will eventually find out they are just as ordinary as everyone else and may not be worthy of the recognition and income.

Take a moment now to think about those things that create fear in you. What do you imagine could hold you back? What do you know for sure are things you need to work on before you get started? Are you prepared to work through them? Are you determined enough to overcome them?

If you want to achieve your goals in this business, you will need to understand these fears and work to conquer them. You must realize that the only way to work through your fears and banish them is to do the very thing you fear. Do it over and over again until you no longer fear it. This is not easy. It will take time and perseverance. But the rewards in overcoming your fears and the success it will bring you in this business are worth it.

If you fear prospecting, you're going to have to get out there and prospect. If you fear sharing your product, you will have to get out there and share your product. If you are mortified by the idea of speaking in front of a group of people, then guess what? You are going to have to get up and speak in front of a group of people. You aren't going to be perfect the first time you do it. It could take ten, twenty, even fifty times until you do what you need to do with more confidence, a lot less fear, and with a level of competence. However, the improvement in your self-esteem and the raising of your self-confidence is well worth the attempt.

Overcoming your fears is not something you need to do alone. This is a benefit of working with a group of people who are all working in partnership. You are all on a similar path with similar goals, part of the same vehicle. Not only will you be in league with many team members who share your journey and feel the way you do, but you have access to leaders who have often overcome what you need to and can mentor you to success.

Make sure you take advantage of their experience and wisdom. Share what you are feeling, and make sure you take in what you need to work your way forward. There is no fear in this business that has not been struggled with in the past and overcome. Not one. Whatever you are going through, or whatever you expect to arise, you should be confident that someone in your company has also worked through it, and you can too.

Staying Positive and Focused

Whether you are building a network marketing business or setting up the hottest new enterprise, you must find a way to stay focused, stay positive, and eliminate distractions. Staying positive is a must, as you will soon realize that business—any business—has its ups and downs. Not everything will go your way, and you will need to be mentally ready for that. Being optimistic is a must, and in network marketing you have a great need for optimism because you never know what is about to happen in your business. You don't know where or when your next leader is coming from. You could struggle to find someone today, then tomorrow, by a chance meeting, you recruit the next big income earner in your company.

 Fact

Vision boards are a powerful way to focus on your goals. Pin photos of things that you are working toward, such as a new car or vacation in Spain, onto a bulletin board. Place the board somewhere you will see it as often as possible. Your mind will work in amazing ways to help get you closer to what appears on your board.

This is one of the most exciting aspects of network marketing—the never-ending potential for massive change. Just one sale, one new person in your business, can improve everything in a split second. A new state or country being launched, a new product released, a successful leader decides to join your team . . . there are many things that could suddenly create a spark and the next wave of growth in your business. You just have to stay positive and believe it can happen to you.

Staying positive is not only important for you, but it is crucial in supporting your team. They want to see you as an optimistic leader who is pursuing a vision with a confidence that it will be achieved. They want to be able to call you when they are feeling down, knowing full well they are going to be encouraged and lifted by your positive outlook in where the company and their business is headed. Is it easy to stay positive all the time? Of course not. But it is a characteristic you can work on and eventually make a natural part of your personality.

As you spend more time with top leaders in your company, you'll begin to notice that they are always optimistic, always positive, always sure that the best is ahead. It won't be long before that vibe rubs off on you as well, and your own team begins to notice the difference.

 Alert

> If your actions and results aren't inspiring others to follow you, you need to work on your leadership skills. The best way is to look at the leaders in your company you would like to be like and start to apply much of the way they accomplish their business-building activities.

Staying focused is definitely one of the most difficult functions in this business to achieve. Just think of your life right now. It would be fair to say that, like most people, you have a lot happening. A combination of a job, family, sports activities, and socializing has made sure that most people in today's society are feeling busy, and even overwhelmed in some cases, from the time they open their eyes to the minute they crash into bed, fatigued both mentally and physically.

In fact, lack of energy is a major complaint with most people as we struggle to complete the abundance of tasks that are placed before us on a daily basis. This is where the need for disciplined focus comes in. If you are serious about making this business work, you will need to find a way to block out a portion of your week, ideally ten to fifteen hours, where you will focus on building your business. This is a commitment to your success. It's also a commitment to your team and your family.

Distractions and events that will make you lose focus will come at you from all directions. Your child may want you at tonight's football game just as your company's webinar is about to begin. Your father calls and asks for help in starting his car ten minutes before your meeting with a high-level prospect. You're about to give your first testimonial on your team conference call when Uncle Bob from Florida calls just minutes earlier to have his yearly catch-up call.

 Alert

A recent study conducted by Microsoft found that the average attention span is now just eight seconds, down from twelve in the year 2000.

There are dozens of ways you can be thrown off course, but you must develop the discipline to get back on. Your life will never be a blank slate, open to simply pursuing your business with nothing else to focus on. There will always be something else. There will always be another option. You have to work to shut those things out of your mind and focus on what needs to be done to drive your business forward.

Spend some time planning out a timetable of when you will be working your business. Let your family know. Have a place set aside where business is conducted, even if it is your kitchen table. If there are things close by that distract you, such as the television being on or your computer screen with Facebook open, it may be best to either find another place to work or turn them off. This is such a vital part of building your business. Staying focused, just for short periods of time, will accelerate your success and give you a discipline that will flow into other areas of your life.

Dealing with Procrastination

We are all prone to putting things off until later, when we may "feel" like doing them. Procrastination is an issue you not only need to deal with in your personal life, but it's also a behavior you will need to address in building a business.

As you build your business, you will find a variety of reasons to postpone doing what needs to be done. It's going to take a lot of discipline and focus to work through it. Perhaps the easiest way to stay focused on the rewards and benefits of completing a task is to create a vision board of all the things you see yourself buying, doing, and accomplishing. Think of the increase in your commission and what you will be able to afford. Think of the climb to the next promotion in your compensation plan and see yourself walk across the stage to receive an award. Some people have even claimed that they got no other benefit other than taking items off their to-do list, which helped them sleep better.

The rewards differ for everyone. Whatever those rewards are, you must keep in mind that they will only arrive when you create results through action. The more you procrastinate, the further you push those rewards away.

When You Need to Bounce Back

No matter how much planning you put forward, no matter how much support you get, and no matter how good your team is, there are going to be times when things don't go the way you want them to:

- A favorite product is suddenly out of stock.
- Your best leader quits and joins another program.

- A negative piece of news about your company makes it into the media.

Sometimes the causes have nothing to do with the business itself but are issues related to your own personal life. Problems with your children at school, your spouse, or your daytime job may hamper your attitude and make you feel that you can't focus on your network marketing business. This is not uncommon. It happens to new people as well as those with decades of experience in the business. Several factors can affect your mood, drive down your confidence, and have you questioning whether you are doing the right thing.

You can overcome this by having a plan of action for when you feel like this. You can't always depend on just snapping out of it. That could take more time than what you can afford, and it is not a reliable way to walk through any predicament.

Network marketing offers you the support of other people who have either gone through what you are feeling or can lead you to someone that has. Your upline and company have a vested interest in your success. Your success in this business helps everyone. They are not only concerned with what you are going through, but they're also ready to provide help when you need it. When you need a boost, your sponsor and leaders in your upline should be the first point of contact in order to begin the rejuvenation process.

 Alert

> Never contact members of your downline when you are feeling negative. They will sense your lack of enthusiasm and belief, and may begin to wonder if you're the leader they should be working with. Contact your downline when you are feeling good, and reach out to your upline when you need a mental boost. Never complain to your downline. Always take your complaints and feelings upline.

As you continue building your business, you will become aware of this fluctuation in your feelings. Here are several ways you can work your way out of an unexpected rut and get back to being your best.

- **Contact your sponsor/upline:** Get on the phone or meet up for coffee. Let them know your concerns and why they are present. Your sponsor may offer a different point of view or share an idea you may not have implemented yet.
- **Contact your corporate team:** Most companies will have a corporate team that is eager and willing to interact with field members. They want to hear from you and help you succeed. Don't hesitate to make a call to your regional manager or vice president of sales in your market.
- **Attend company/team events:** The excitement, camaraderie, and optimism that comes with an event cannot be underestimated. Companies and leaders understand this and place a great emphasis on getting people to major events. If you have yet to attend a company event or haven't been to one in a while, it may be time to get your tickets.
- **Participate in online webinars or team conference calls:** These calls could be weekly or monthly, and some teams even have a daily pep call. The interaction with leaders in your company and hearing other people succeeding may be just what you need at this point in time.
- **Watch company video updates:** Many companies are now implementing weekly or monthly video updates for their reps. Not only will you hear about messages directly from the company, but you will see other reps sharing positive messages that just may help you make the switch and fire up your enthusiasm.
- **Seek out positive messages:** There are thousands of books that can help you get motivated and inspired to

get back into action. Your upline are sure to have many suggestions. Also be sure to search YouTube for hundreds of uplifting videos that can get you back in the groove. Favorites are videos from Les Brown and Tony Robbins, as well as Art Williams' "Just Do It" speech.

- **Listen to music:** Music can often help you change the way you feel. Uplifting, inspiring music or songs that remind you of when you were at your best can be kept in your MP3 player or phone, and you can play them when needed to help change the way you are feeling.

Sometimes all you need is a breather—a chance to stand back and evaluate where you're at. You may be feeling overwhelmed or have taken on too many tasks in a short period of time. Don't be afraid to admit you just need a day or two, sometimes even a week, to rest up and come back refreshed a few days later.

CHAPTER 12

Growing Your Team

You can definitely earn a few hundred or even a couple thousand dollars a month in network marketing simply by retailing products or services. But if you want to achieve higher income levels, get recognized on stage for your promotions, or create true residual earnings, you will need to learn how to grow and support a team of like-minded reps. A unique aspect of network marketing, unlike similar sales structures, is that you don't recruit people, train them, and risk them becoming your competitor. In this industry, you recruit, train, and then enter a long-term partnership with mutual benefits.

Creating a Prospect List

A prospect list is a record of names of people you would like to approach about either joining your team or using your products. This is a very important step, and it should be one of the very first things you begin working on once you start your business.

Just start writing down the names of everyone you know, and never assume to know whether your prospect is interested or not. Thoughts like "John is a doctor, so he won't be interested," or "I know Linda is wealthy; this won't be for her" are the kinds of decisions that can cost you tens of thousands of dollars down the road. So don't prejudge; just get down the names.

On your list will likely be several people who have the potential to be strong leaders in your organization, a few who are looking to supplement their income with a few hundred dollars a month, and many who are not looking to start a business but want to benefit from using your services. You don't know who slots into each category.

 Fact

> You many find yourself initially struggling to compile a prospect list, but you probably already have a great one. Jot down every name you have in your phone's contacts list or through social media.

Don't make the mistake of having five or six people "in your head" who you think will be ready to join your team. This is one of the most common mistakes new reps make. They fail to have a big enough list, and they neglect to put that list on paper. If you think the first handful of people you approach are going to be interested enough to join, you're going to be disappointed. Make sure you get down at least 100–200 names, contact them, and then allow them to determine whether they want to find out more or not.

Start with those people who are already on your phone's contacts list, then add in those you know through social media like Facebook, LinkedIn, and Twitter. Many of these people could have a real need for either your business or product.

If you have friends, relatives, or business associates based either in other states or overseas, be sure you also place them on your list. Check your company's website and look to see in what states and countries your company is doing business. Whether you contact them on the phone or online, make sure you don't miss out on this often neglected opportunity to expand your business outside the area you live.

Remember that your mission is to share your business (not sell the business!) to people looking for the same things you are: a better lifestyle, greater income, the benefits of superior products and services. Your job is not to convince people, argue with them, or twist their arm in order to join you.

 Essential

Plan to get at least 100 names on your first prospect list of family and friends. Be sure to include all your relatives that may be living in other states or overseas in countries that your company is open in.

Don't be emotionally tied to their decision. Most people say they want success but aren't willing to do the work it requires. So don't worry about how many say "No," "Maybe," or "I'll get back to you later." You're looking for the serious people that want to do something with their lives today.

Your prospect list is an ever-changing document, with prospects being removed as they either join your business or say no and new prospects added on a regular basis. These prospects can come about through focused efforts to add to the list, or you may be someone who easily strikes up conversations with people and is able to obtain their details.

 Alert

Instill a level of urgency when it comes to developing and contacting people on your prospect list. Stories abound of people who held off on contacting a prospect and then found their prospect had joined someone else in the same company who contacted the prospect just days or even hours earlier.

Don't feel the need to prospect everyone you meet, or feel obligated to add them to your list. Some people, due to personality clashes or negative attitudes, may never be right for your business—or may be right for the business but wrong for your team culture. It's a feature of network marketing that you get to choose whom you want to work with, rather than being lumped with a group of people you struggle to tolerate.

Developing a large list of people doesn't mean you are obligated to sponsor all of them. Your only role is to simply give them the opportunity to look at what you are working on; then leave it to them to determine if it is right for them or not.

Contacting and Inviting

If you seriously want to succeed in network marketing, you have to be able to get out there and meet people. Nothing happens in this business until someone buys something from another individual, and that won't happen if you are not proactive in sharing your opportunity and products.

If you truly like working by yourself—analyzing numbers, inputting data, or trading in the stock market—you may not find the social aspect of network marketing to your liking. This is a people business. If you find people annoying and difficult to work with, contacting them and inviting them to look at your business is probably not something you are going to do well with.

This doesn't mean you will need to be the stereotypical happy-go-lucky, life-of-the-party type. Many, many introverts have succeeded in network marketing. You will, however, need to be a little outgoing, able to hold a decent conversation with new people, and develop a generally positive outlook on life. Not many people want to join someone who has a pessimistic attitude.

Once you have developed your list, it's time to use your social skills to your advantage, contacting every individual one by one in order to make an invitation. This is where a simple script, usually developed by your company, will be a major asset. You should never begin an invitation call by ad-libbing, with no prior preparation. Being aware of what you are going to say before you need to say it will help you appear confident in what you are promoting. "The less you say, the more you make."

Also be sure, whenever possible, to do your invitations over the phone. You can do this while at home, relaxing in a pool, or taking your morning walk. The most important part is that they are done over the phone. That way you can stick to time limits for how long you stay in conversation with the prospect. You can do the call while in a convenient location that suits you. And you can cut the call short if the prospect decides to get into irrelevant details regarding what you are doing and why. These tips will also help improve your success with your invitation. If you're afraid of making phone calls, a great read by Tammy Stanley, a network marketing trainer, is *Carpe Phonum: How to Seize the Phone, Take Action and Call Your Prospects, Even When You Lack Courage.*

- **Clear the time:** Ask the prospect if she has two minutes free right now. If she says no, respect that and ask when it would be a better time to call. If she is okay to talk, then respect the fact that you only asked for two minutes of her time.
- **Have a scripted invitation:** You need to know what you're going to say, and practice, practice, practice that invitation until you are reading it clearly and with authority. If you stumble over the words or say them mechanically, you're going to have your prospect focusing more on how you are speaking rather than the information you are sharing.
- **Stick to the purpose of your call:** You're calling your prospect to see if he is open to looking at an opportunity to make more money or try your product. Don't get the both of you distracted with discussions about the weather, the Super Bowl, or what Sarah wrote on Facebook. There are times for social chats; this is not one of them.
- **It's an invitation call, not a sign-up call:** Don't make the mistake of trying to sponsor people on your first call.

They will never know enough about the business from one call, and may make assumptions about how it works that leads them to say no. It's an invitation to take a look, not an invitation to get started.

- **It's an invitation call, not a presentation call:** Don't make the mistake of giving a presentation about the entire business, company, comp plan, owners, and on and on. This is not the time. Know the difference between the invitation and the presentation. The presentation is saved for later, after the prospect says yes to the invitation. That is when you show the video or take the prospect to a business opportunity presentation.

- **Be prepared with the next step:** This is a common mistake, usually caused by being unprepared. A representative will call, excited to invite the prospect to look at the business, but when the prospect says yes, the rep doesn't proceed to the next step in the process and offer something to look at. Talk to your sponsor and ask, "When my prospect says yes, what do I show her?"

It's important that you get a large number of people looking at your business to ensure you get enough of a team developing from the beginning so you can get momentum right away. After your first couple of months of exposing your business to as many prospects as you can, you can then settle into exposing a few people a week on a consistent basis. This will keep your network growing solidly and help keep you qualified for commissions in a compensation plan that may require you to personally sponsor every month to achieve leadership bonuses.

Try to always use tools (websites, videos, CDs) to then share your opportunity, so you can save time and create leverage. Remember, this is a business that is most often built part-time, so it's important that you let the tools do the work of sharing information with your prospect.

Think about how you were invited to the business and what information you were asked to look at. In all likelihood, that same information you viewed will appeal to your prospects too. Get hold of whatever it was and begin to use that tool as part of your own prospecting.

 Essential

Treat people online as you would offline. Don't send out mass spam messages or group postings, but do initiate conversations with people that you have a relationship with. Get their permission first before you share your information.

Don't pressure people to view your presentation. Ask them to take a look; don't ask them to join on the spot. They will most likely put up a defense and offer you reasons why they would not be interested or even suitable for the business. Your best strategy is to invite them to take a look at a presentation and then allow them to decide if it's for them or not.

Making Your Presentation

If your invitation has been made correctly and your prospect is open to checking out your business, it's now time to provide her with a presentation. This could be related to your business or just the products or service. It's usually a better idea to show a full presentation combining both at first and allow her to decide which part of the presentation appeals to her the most.

The most essential factor in your presentation is that you use third-party tools. By using professionally produced material, you can showcase your opportunity without actually making the whole presentation. It means you don't have to spend time memorizing dozens of facts and figures, and more importantly, you become the messenger, not the message. That is where you will get the most duplication long-term. By ignoring this strategy, you will not only stifle duplication, but you will create reasons for your prospect to not feel competent enough to join your business.

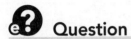 **Question**

What do I do if my company has no professional presentation available yet?
Your sponsor, a leader in your team, or a corporate member can all be used as third-party resources. If your sponsor is doing all the talking, and you and your prospect are doing the listening, your prospect will understand that he can do the same thing once he gets started.

Remember that your prospect will be closely watching what you do to present the business, in part to see if it is something she is comfortable doing. If you meet in a coffee shop for your presentation, then spend an hour verbally relaying every aspect of your compensation plan, unique products, and history of your CEO, she may end up being impressed, but more with your memory than the opportunity. She may think that in order to make the business work, she'll need to remember what coding bonuses are paid on your third generation, why iron is added to your Mega-Mix pack but not the Fortified Friday Mix, and how your CEO was actually born in the same hospital as Donald Trump.

If you have spent sixty minutes reciting your monologue, she will subconsciously assume that this is what she needs to do to also present the business. No matter how excited she is by your opportunity, she will start to wonder whether she can remember everything you shared. Rather than risking the embarrassment of trying to remember all the key points you mentioned, she will opt to continue in another direction.

Leaders in the industry who are great at public speaking have also been caught in this trap. Many have invited their prospect to a hotel meeting where they are the speaker giving the presentation and end up with a prospect who believes he will also need to become a great public speaker in order to make the business work for him.

To succeed in prospecting, you must be aware of the fact that how you present your opportunity is what your prospect believes she will be doing. If at the end of each presentation you hear, "You're going to do really well with this, but it's not for me," you can be sure that the fault lies in your method of presenting.

Tools—such as company DVDs, CDs, a website, or online video—work well because people are more confident in sharing a presentation rather than performing one themselves. This book, for example, could be used as a tool for prospects who want more information on how the business works before they join your team. The company's website can be used by anyone who wants to find out more about the company's corporate team. A product brochure can be handed out that can educate your prospect on why your heat patches work so effectively. Anything you can use to do the explaining for you, rather than you having to remember the details and making the presentation verbally, is a much more effective way to grow your business.

Successful Follow-Up

Most people, no matter how impressed they are with your product, want time to look over what you have presented and will only make a decision once they have read all the facts and figures.

It's important that you take the initiative with your prospects and follow up to see what decision they have made. No matter how positive they are to get started, it is not necessarily the norm to have your prospects call you back first, hurriedly asking you to sign up. If you sit back, present your business, then hope a prospect is going to call you and ask to join, then you are in for a long wait and a slow-growing business. Remember that the "fortune is in the follow-up."

Following up is not just a skill; it is an intentional act combined with discipline. There is no room for procrastination, as every day you put off contacting the prospect to either get an answer or clarify his questions is twenty-four hours closer to him losing interest in your opportunity.

You know that life gets in the way for most people. The things they were enthusiastic about last week are today forgotten. Your prospects are no different. Once they have seen your presentation, make sure they understand that you will be in touch soon to get their response and answer any questions or objections. Then they not only understand that part of the process, but they expect it. If you are not following up in a consistent manner, you can be sure your prospects will assume that you are not as serious about the business as you appeared.

 Alert

Always follow up less than twenty-four hours after a presentation, so the prospect knows you are building your team with urgency and are excited to have him in it. Nothing can kill the process faster than letting a contact grow cold, so don't forget to make that phone call!

Following up is not just about hassling the prospect until he says yes. It is done with respect, at mutually agreed times, with the purpose of discovering whether a partnership together in your company will work out for the best. It's also an opportunity to provide the prospect with more resources that will allow him to further his research and gather more information in his own space and time.

Remember, you are not there to hassle a prospect into joining you; you simply respectfully ask if she wants to be part of your team or wants to use the products or service as a customer. Your job is not to convince a prospect of what is right or wrong; your job is to invite him to look, then to follow up and collect a decision.

Don't be shy about asking for referrals from those who are not interested in the business or your products. Every person you know can provide you with at least five to ten new contacts. If they like your products and see you as a professional, they will gladly provide those names.

Just make sure you don't abuse their trust. They are providing you with a list of their friends and acquaintances. They gave you the names because they felt they could trust you. Don't abuse that trust by trying to "hard-sell" these contacts.

Closing the Deal

While people often use the phrase "closing the deal" when it comes to sales, that phrase, when it comes to network marketing, requires a different understanding. In this industry you are not "closing" people, but rather "opening" them to new beginnings.

In traditional sales, you would close the sale once you have reached the end of the process and the prospect has agreed to make a purchase of goods or services from you or your company.

 Alert

Don't risk family tensions by hard-selling your family. You may get the sale but lose out on your personal goals in the long run. If they don't buy from you today, they may change their minds once you are more successful. No doesn't necessarily mean no, it may mean "not now."

In network marketing, this is where the process actually truly begins. The invitation, the presentation, the follow-up, and the submitted application are all a prelude to a greater objective: to create and maintain a long-term business partnership with the mutual goal of growing a successful organization and satisfied product customers.

To reach this point in the process, your prospect would have reviewed your material, analyzed the business, tried the products, and had his questions answered. He will then make a decision as to whether it meets his lifestyle and income needs by being part of your opportunity.

If you have followed the guidelines set out in this book, shown respect for his decision-making, and made sure that he doesn't feel pressured into signing up, you will find yourself with a greater chance of obtaining a positive response.

Duplication

"Duplication" is commonly defined as making an exact copy of something. In network marketing, the concept of duplication refers to copying and applying an effective method of operation, and it plays an important role in building a huge organization. The fastest-growing, most solid organizations in this industry have emerged when team members are using the same system to grow their business.

It is a concept borrowed from the franchising business model, tweaked to fit a business model that is occasionally referred to as the "people's franchise." A system will usually be created and put in place by the leaders in your organization, often in conjunction with company sales executives. A good system will outline how to prospect for new team members, how to develop a group of customers, what to use when presenting your opportunity, and how and when to follow up with prospects. Most systems are flexible enough to adjust to different situations, but in general they help you cover what you need to do on a daily, weekly, monthly, and sometimes even yearly basis.

If a system works very well, it will help create success for those that choose to follow it. In a strong, duplication-focused organization, it will become quite easy to see who is following the system and who isn't. In building their business, some reps unknowingly leave out the very things they need the most. The man who most needs to work on his personal development will not take part in the team leadership program, or the woman who complains about a lack of communication never takes part in the weekly company webinar. These people often refuse to participate in the activities they need the most in order to prosper. They will also be the first to highlight that nobody in their team is working their business, which is a problem that stems from the leader not following and teaching a system that duplicates.

Once you have understood and learned to implement your team's system, the easier it will be for you to identify who is not following it and help them get on track. It's been said that the golden rule to success in this business is to get a large group of people to do a few simple things over a sustained period of time. This is the essence of what a good system will allow you to do. Be consistent and persistent over time to get results.

The building blocks of a system must be based on simplicity, with actions that can be followed by every person that is a part of your organization. If you introduce activities that are difficult to apply or achieve positive results with, the system will fail and will need to be rapidly adjusted. If your system is too rigid and detailed, it will be difficult to duplicate, resulting in most people not following it. If your system is too flexible and open to constant change, confidence in the system will wane and team members will begin to feel free to tailor it to suit their own interests.

Here's an example of a very simple system that was implemented by one organization several years ago:

1. Use the products or services daily, weekly; be a product of the products.
2. Complete at least thirty minutes of personal development daily.

3. Stay connected. Be on the weekly conference call and view the monthly corporate video.
4. Attend all local events, and the major regional events. You might not think you can afford to, but the reality is, you can't afford *not* to.
5. Introduce your business, product, or service to at least two people a day.

Too simple? Not detailed enough? Perhaps. But keep in mind, you don't need a highly sophisticated plan in order to create solid duplication. The more complex your plan, the less chance it has of being duplicated by your team.

Finally, as with much of what you do in network marketing, sit down with your sponsor to get a good grounding in what your system is and how you should apply it. Most organizations will have their system documented in either a small booklet or a PDF that can be downloaded.

 Fact

In the back of every prospect's mind are two questions when it comes to giving a presentation: "Can I do this?" and "Would I want this done to people I know?" The more hype-filled and difficult your presentation is, the more likely the prospect will say no to the business.

If you see others succeed with a system, don't be overconfident and think you can create your own or modify the one being used. Learn the one your upline is using, utilize it, and teach it to your team. Don't reinvent the wheel. A good, strong system is the basis of duplication, and solid duplication is the key to a lifetime of ongoing income in network marketing.

CHAPTER 13

Supporting Your Team

As you begin to form an organization bursting with representatives and customers, it is imperative that you have systems and practices in place to help provide support, increase retention of your business builders, and create an environment that people are happy to be part of. A lack of support is often cited as the major reason team members leave the industry, an issue you will need to address if you want to build a thriving business that appeals to both full-time and part-time reps.

Training Your Recruits

Signing an application and taking a spot in your compensation plan is just the beginning. It is now absolutely important that your new recruit is given the right training in launching a successful network marketing business.

A starter kit or welcome pack will usually follow once the recruit is signed up, allowing her to begin the preliminary training process just days after beginning. Many companies will even have in place online training that can be accessed the moment she joins your business.

Be sure you make her aware of any resources she can go through in those first forty-eight hours, as this is usually the period where new team members can be unsure of whether the business will work for them and if they are doing the right thing.

Your company and upline can also provide you with the educational materials on everything from the compensation plan to why and how your products were created. This is a crucial period in her networking career, and it is now up to you to transfer the belief you have about your business into her heart and mind. This needs to be done with passion, enthusiasm, and a lot of patience.

 Alert

If your new team member won't take the time to do the initial training, she is probably going to struggle in this business. Reps who make the effort in learning what they have to do and why develop greater belief in their decision to get involved in network marketing.

Be sure to take advantage of any events that are coming up where you can take her to see the bigger picture. There is nothing that will instill belief in her decision faster than being in a room of like-minded people who are excited about their new opportunity. Giving your new team members the proper environment in order for them to learn the skills and attitudes required will help lay the foundations of a flourishing organization.

Communication

Good business, just like a good relationship, hinges on great communication. While we know effective communication is important in large corporate settings, many people forget that it can be even more important in other types of business—network marketing being no exception. You will need to communicate well with your downline, your upline, your customers, and even your corporate team.

Good communication begins with being aware of what is happening in your business. Don't get stuck on the treadmill of "I didn't know" and "You didn't tell me." Your downline will begin to question your commitment and may think that you don't care about the business or them.

You may be doing a lot behind the scenes in terms of support and laying strong foundations, but if you don't communicate what you are working on and why, you will rapidly see a slowdown in your progress and a lack of confidence in your leadership.

To understand what your team desires regarding good communication, ask yourself what would help you stay on top of what you need to know. Is it a weekly e-mail update? A short video posted on the team's site? A private Facebook group Page? A weekly conference call? In all likelihood, those things that you feel would be helpful to you are also of interest to your team members. Whichever forms of communication you and the company choose to use, be sure you are consistently providing everyone an opportunity to stay up to date.

Using Social Media for Team Support

Social media, which includes Facebook, YouTube, Google+, and many similar sites and applications, makes it easier than ever for you to support and motivate your team. From a like on a Facebook post to a well-worded Tweet, you can now use a variety of methods to make sure every team member in your group feels he or she is part of a family.

If a team member reaches a new level in your business, be sure to be one of the first to send your congratulations via the site he uses the most. If he's made a valuable contribution on a webinar or conference call, let him know so that others can also read your message and join in the support.

Almost every company has a Facebook business Page, allowing a company to keep all its subscribers updated with relevant information. You can also set up a private group Page on Facebook where you can recognize your high achievers, welcome new team members, and provide business-building ideas.

⊜! Alert

While supporting your team via social media is highly effective and encouraged, you shouldn't avoid picking up the phone and having a good conversation when possible. If you spend all your time sending private messages through Facebook Messenger, for example, your team member may get the feeling you are avoiding talking to him for some unknown reason.

Rewards and Recognition

Many people stay in the business for the recognition and the sense of belonging. Network marketing organizations do an incredible job of providing an environment where people feel welcomed and accepted. And they go out of their way to have even the smallest step forward by a team member acknowledged and duly rewarded.

Most people are motivated by praise and awards. When it comes to recognition, it's been said that babies cry for it and grown men die for it. Smart organizations recognize this and have set up multiple ways in which achievers in their business are praised for their accomplishments. From a gold pin that can be placed on a jacket lapel to an extra cash bonus awarded at the company convention, companies are constantly looking at ways to uniquely recognize those who get out of their comfort zone and hit a special goal or overcome a personal obstacle.

Your personal team will also look to you to provide this recognition and praise. This is one area where you cannot afford to be stingy. The more you genuinely compliment and cheer on your team, the more eager they will be to reach that next level—to talk to that next person—to see more potential customers.

 Question

I'd like to offer better rewards, but I am on a tight budget. What else can I do?
Keep in mind that not all rewards need to be material goods. Your company will provide most of those. If the best you can do initially is a phone call offering your congratulations, or a dinner with your whole group where each person pitches in for the team member being recognized, this is a great way to start.

Don't simply assume that because your company pays them a commission and is recognizing your team with pins and certificates that they won't appreciate more from you. You will in fact be surprised to find that many of them will do more to earn this type of recognition than they will to earn their bonuses. Many companies publish a monthly recognition list of those who have achieved certain targets in the compensation plan. If you could ask many of these achievers, you will probably find that they were more excited in having been seen on the list than in what their commission was that month. This only underscores how much you will need to focus on a process that allows you to spot who is doing well in your organization and what rewards should be given for their achievement.

When Art Williams first launched insurance giant A.L. Williams & Associates in the late 1970s (today known as Primerica), he was so acutely aware of the recognition factor that he would hand out T-shirts with motivational slogans printed on them to many of his representatives. It was not long before many new reps would make it their sole goal to earn the T-shirt and have it handed over by Art himself at the next company event. Coffee company and network marketing giant Organo Gold famously implemented its own version of a "knighting," where leaders who had proven their determination, hard work, and vision were invited to take part in a public ceremony highlighting their new status and welcoming them into an exclusive inner circle of successful representatives.

 Fact

Sometimes the best way to help encourage your new team member is by getting her to an event. She'll meet others who are involved in the business and can be introduced to members of your upline who can offer support.

How you choose to recognize your team is only limited by your imagination. It's best to work with your sponsor to map out how you intend to make it happen, and then make sure you provide the rewards and accolades that are deserved when they are due.

Dealing with Difficult People

Network marketing is a people business. You will be dealing with people in your team, in your family, and in the head office whether it is distributor service or corporate executives. People being people, you will already understand that not everyone you come across will instantly connect with you. Good rapport will not automatically develop the moment you sit with a new prospect.

Sometimes, no matter how hard you try with some people, and no matter how patient you are, there will be reps and customers you won't get along with. Almost everything they do will rub you the wrong way, and even minor things will begin to make it difficult to work with them.

An advantage of network marketing is that you will receive plenty of counseling and support in learning how to deal with all manners of people. Those who immersed themselves in the personal development that comes as part of this industry have often found themselves much more understanding and tolerant of what you may see initially as a difficult person. It doesn't mean they go away; it just means that the way you handle them is better.

One difficult person can surely ruin your day if you choose to allow it, so why not develop the attitude and skills to make sure a difficult person isn't able to do that? Here are some valuable tips you can use immediately to tame the most difficult of people to work with.

- **Listen.** A common reason people may appear to be difficult is that they don't feel the person they are talking to is listening to them. You can validate someone's concerns by sincerely listening to what she is saying.
- **Show empathy.** Try to put yourself in his shoes. Do your best to see the situation from his point of view. You may not agree with his stance, but understanding it will make him feel heard.
- **Ask questions.** Simply nodding your head or staring into her eyes is not enough. Add in a question that helps clarify what she is saying, even if it means she has to repeat her words. She will still value your interest in her thoughts.
- **Find a connection.** You may both have been born in Idaho or share an interest in European coins. The more you can work to find a bond with him, the more likely he will see you as a friend than an enemy.
- **Bring in a third party.** He may not respect you, but he may highly respect someone that knows you. Use this to influence him in keeping his behavior in check, particularly if you feel an argument or even physical violence could take place.
- **Don't sink to her level.** Her difficulties may stem from being overly cynical and negative toward every possi-

ble situation. You can listen to these concerns, but you should not agree with them. She is looking for solutions, not someone stuck in the same boat she is.

- **Work toward a positive result.** No matter how forceful he becomes in swerving you off your course, take the higher ground and focus on an end result that will ultimately benefit the both of you.

As you become more proficient in dealing with difficult people, you will notice that it gets easier to work out their traits and personality quirks. This business will throw at you everything from the guy who can't see why he has to pay to attend an event to the lady who wants to call team members and berate them for dressing too casually at the last function. If you are going to pursue a long-term career in network marketing, you're going to have to learn to deal with all that and everything in between. Don't take that as a negative and something to avoid. By the time you have reached the higher levels in your compensation plan, you will have a knack for diplomacy that even the cleverest politicians could only wish for.

Success through Teamwork

You can't get to a high level of income by only selling the products yourself. You can't build a large, thriving organization by sponsoring every team member yourself. And you definitely should not achieve higher levels in your compensation plan by purchasing the required volume of products or services yourself.

This business is a team activity. Its rewards come through building a team. Its security comes in building a team. While there are definitely businesses available where you can work alone, this is not one of them.

Network marketing has no place for anybody with a "my way or the highway" attitude. And it swiftly deals with those who come in with know-it-all behavior, ego, or a huge arrogance. The sooner you adjust your thinking to working within a team structure built around support, recognition, and encouragement, the faster you will see growth and results.

 Essential

Many of your team members may have certain skills and characteristics that will complement your own or fill a requirement needed by your team. You may not be great at public speaking or writing a newsletter, but you may find team members that are accomplished at both.

Begin to look for ways you can be more of a team player and activities that can help foster a feeling of teamwork within your organization. One of the worst things you can do is act indifferent to your team or act like you are better than them. Remember, never forget where you came from.

They want you to spend time with them, to encourage them and offer them your support in reaching their goals. If you appear to them as if you are going it alone, you can be sure they will pick up on that and eventually choose to work with another leader who values their company and efforts.

Encouragement and Inspiration

Having your team members know they have your support and encouragement at every turn will do wonders for their confidence. They want to be sure that they will be acknowledged for their efforts and that someone is paying close attention to their achievements, no matter how small they may appear.

A successful network marketer strives to understand different people's style and temperament. You will listen to their concerns and support their dreams. You may encounter people who are initially difficult to work with, or have challenges in understanding different aspects of the business, but over time you will learn how to overcome these issues. People skills are the key in helping you in these areas, and working with people must become a daily part of your business development.

You need to be the first contact when your team members are promoted and let them know how happy you are for them. Cheer them on through social media, adding your own comments and liking items that pertain to areas of their life that are important to them. Uplift and use them as inspiration for others to see what is possible. You're the greatest cheerleader they have and they know it!

 Essential

Just as in any form of sales, your new team member can often get cold feet in those first few days and even hours after making her decision to join. This is where you need to focus and make sure she understands she made a great decision by building up her belief level.

A combination of recognition by both the company and your own team will help create an environment where every team member is encouraged to grow and succeed. Naturally there will be some in your organization who need more of a push, who need more self-confidence and belief. Your role is to be the facilitator for both, to help initiate the path your team members can take to move forward and overcome their mental barriers. Use your company events. Use an inspirational online movie. Get them to a special gathering with achievers in your company. A good leader will develop a collection of ways to help a team member produce a breakthrough.

One company recently developed a series of online audios where successful reps shared their story of how they got started and what they had to do to overcome their frustrations in order to succeed. They made these audios available for free and download-able to both team members and prospects, allowing them to be encouraged by these inspiring testimonials.

You will have your own unique ways to support and motivate your team. It may be as simple as sending them an exciting e-mail or inviting them to spend time with a leader flying in from another country. The opportunities to create inspiring messages that move your team forward are endless. Focus on your team, take notice of things that inspire them, and then get to work and create unique and stimulating activities or messages that will help motivate them into action.

CHAPTER 14

Retailing Your Product or Service

There will often be times when your prospect has no interest in taking part in a business, but is enthusiastic about using your product. This offers you the opportunity to create a new retail customer who uses your products due to a genuine interest in their quality and effectiveness. A small group of retail customers does more than just provide increased sales volume. A satisfied customer, well taken care of, can often be your best advocate and a source of new prospects.

The Benefits of Retailing

Retailing product, in its simplest and most commonly applied form, is accomplished by purchasing a product at a wholesale cost, then selling the product to an end user with a markup that helps cover incidental costs and allows you to create a profit. This markup, or retail profit, is often already recommended by your company, with the retail cost of the product listed in your catalog or a price list that can be viewed by your customer.

Becoming proficient in retailing your product will help increase sales volume and open new circles of potential customers and people who may be interested in becoming reps. Many team members love this aspect of the business. They enjoy the process of highlighting product features to a customer and creating a transaction, which helps create immediate income. The retail profit can then be reinvested into the growth of the business, help balance the family budget, or allow you to indulge in a weekly spa and massage. What you do with this extra income is up to you to decide.

 Essential

Remember that your current customers can also be viewed as business prospects. They may become interested in buying more products from you and should always be considered potential team members for your downline.

Satisfied customers who use the product regularly also provide you with an excellent opportunity to gather feedback regarding items your company provides but you may not currently use. If your company sells personal-care products and you're a male distributor, there may be several products available exclusively for women that you probably are not interested in. You may have no desire to use these products yourself, but you should ask your female customers about their experience and perhaps get a testimonial you can then share with other potential buyers.

Proven Ways to Sell Your Product or Service

The absolute first requirement in being able to promote and sell your products or service is using them yourself. If you provide electricity services through your company, but your prospective customer sees your bill coming from XYZ Energy Company, you will have a hard time convincing him you're providing a better option. If you are not using the service yourself, he'll want to know why.

If you are selling a range of vitamins and your friend sees you buying from GNC, then you can be sure that her faith in your product range is not enough for her to make a purchase from you. One network marketing trainer teaches his new team members to go through their kitchen, bathroom, and garage and throw out anything from another retailer that they should be getting from their company. He doesn't want visitors to his home seeing him using an alternative product, nor should you.

Whenever possible, use your product out in public or at home where your friends can see you with it. This works with many energy drinks and portable nutritionals. Make sure you have product on hand whenever someone happens to be in your home. This is often the easiest way to create a new customer. Stirring your friend up a shake or lighting up a scented candle can only happen if you actually have someone in your home. Once she gets a taste of your protein shake, or takes in the aroma of your candles, she will be much more inclined to buy for herself.

Catalog Sales

Catalog selling is a proven way to offer your products, with the Avon, Mary Kay, and Tupperware catalogs being the most recognized. These catalogs are now also available online, and you should check whether your company offers a similar format. If you are using the physical catalog, then be sure you are consistent in distributing them and punctual with your follow-up. You will leave a lot of money on the table if you get the catalogs into your friend's hands but fail to collect her order when she is ready to place it.

Online Retailing

Selling online is a booming part of retailing in network marketing, but you should check with your company's terms and agreement before you plunge into costly websites and complicated online shopping carts. Not every company allows its reps to sell product from an independent online store, mainly to help protect its brand image and help control wild product claims or potentially exorbitant retail prices.

You should also check with your company before selling on sites such as eBay or Craigslist, as not every company allows this form of promotion. Many reps have used their company's trademarks and copyrighted material when selling product through this avenue, and often infringe on their company agreement when doing so.

 Alert

One skin-care company landed in hot water recently when a rep put together before-and-after pictures of a well-known actor using its creams. It was later found the actor had never used the product and that the consultant had created the fake testimonial for promotional purposes without running it by the company.

Your company may already have a replicating retail website currently available that you can take advantage of. This is a better option, as the complicated part of setting up the site and providing payment options are included, and you can be safe in knowing the wording and product claims made on the site are in compliance with company requirements. If your company has this set up for you, not only can you use it to attract more customers, but it can also be used to promote the ease in which your distributors can build a customer base for themselves.

Party-Plan Retailing

One of the oldest, and most popular, ways to retail your product is to hold a sales party. These are easy to organize, can be a lot of fun, and are a great way to create a sizeable retail profit in a short space of time. Rather than seeing ten of your friends one by one over a lengthy period of time, you can invite them all over at one time to relax in your home and sample the products you have available. This works particularly well with products that can be purchased on the spot and experienced while the customers are at your home, such as candles, essential oils, and personal-care products. But you can even hold an in-home business party to inform your guests of the service you are offering, explaining the savings and benefits. At the end of the party for either product or service, you can give a quick invitation for anyone interested in a business opportunity to stay afterward or make another appointment.

 Alert

Your products won't appeal to everybody you come across. Be discerning about which products will interest different people, and don't be aggressive with your promoting when it is obvious the product is not of any relevance to your prospective customer.

Market Stalls, Exhibit Booths, and Trade Shows

Stalls at flea markets can be a very productive way to retail product. Not all products work best with this option, as your customers will usually be interested in something that they can sample on the spot and are relatively inexpensive.

Also be aware that selling certain products at flea markets may downgrade the value of your product range, particularly if you are dealing in a product where prestige and reputation are major selling points. If you choose to go down this route, be sure you have plenty of promotional material on hand, as your buyers will appreciate information on what they have just purchased and how they should most effectively use it, and passersby will often collect a pamphlet or catalog that they can peruse later and decide if they would like to contact you to find out more.

Trade shows can also be a productive way to retail or introduce your service. However, be conscious of not spending too much money to have a booth. Usually, club, school, city, or seasonal fairs are generally cheaper opportunities to market. Anywhere you can be at a place where there are a lot of people at a reasonable price can help further your business. You will also find people that will inquire about your business and eventually may join.

 Alert

Don't use the flea-market method to attract new distributors. Most people will instantly assume that they too will need to sell products at a flea market on a Sunday morning, removing themselves from finding out more about your opportunity.

Conventional Retail Outlets

There are many products in network marketing that fit right into most regular retail environments. While this may appear to conflict with the very need for network marketing in the first place, you should take into account that this avenue should only be used to create a retail sale, not to attract new distributors. Nutritional supplements, essential oils, personal-care products, and skin-care products are items that do well with this method as they are easily placed in most gyms, chiropractic offices, and spas.

If you don't own or manage the store, be respectful and make sure you have the permission from the owner prior to placing your products on the shelves. You also want to organize how sales from your products are attributed to you in terms of profits and not mixed with the business takings at the end of the day. You should also check your company agreement about selling through a retail outlet, as a reason may be stated as to why this method is not permitted by your company.

Preferred Customer Programs

Almost every network marketing company now offers a preferred customer program for retail customers. This is available for prospects who are not interested in building a business but see a need for your product or service and would like to order it at a discounted price.

The company allows you to sign these prospects into your program as preferred customers, and their purchases will then be calculated as part of your sales volume. Any profits that are gained are paid to you as part of your normal commissions.

Preferred customer programs work well because the need to remind the customer to make a purchase is now handled by the company, and special promotions and incentives are offered to your customer directly from the corporate office.

This definitely does not mean you should bring in a preferred customer and totally leave her for the company solely to take care of. No matter how good the customer program is, you should still be in touch with her regularly to make sure she is happy with the products and using them properly. As preferred customer programs differ with every company, be sure to find out how yours works so you can use it when promoting your products.

Increasing Retail Sales

Your best avenue to create increased sales is keeping the customers you currently have satisfied and well serviced. If you are looking after their needs, informing them of new product releases, and helping them create better results with your products, you can be sure that your customers will eventually tell their circle of friends about you. This is the very essence of word-of-mouth marketing.

Create enough trust with your customer so that she is comfortable sharing any concerns she may have (particularly if they are related to health) that can help you identify a product that could help. So many people complain about a lack of energy and focus, but they may only talk about it once they feel comfortable in letting you know. That may be your cue to talk about your energy drink and have her try a sample.

If your product line features many items that she already uses regularly, begin to show comparisons between your products and what she currently buys. You may have a more concentrated dishwashing product that works more effectively and could save her money. You may provide services like gas and electricity, cable, or phone that offer her better value with superior customer service or offer promotional and referral gifts just for trying the service. Products in the home-care area work very well in this regard, with many companies providing quality alternatives to products that people often purchase on a weekly basis regardless of where they have to get it. Also take the time to look around and see which businesses in your area could use your products to complement their present operations.

The car dealership in your suburb may do very well at selling vehicles, but could have a terrible system in place for staying in contact with past and prospective buyers. Could you approach them about your personalized, online greeting card system that will allow sales managers to follow up every few months with a marketing message and brownies attached?

The local mechanic has a thriving business, and his customers are always open to new products to help improve mileage and performance. Could your superior fuel additive become a valuable extension to his product range, giving him an advantage over other mechanics in your area?

The local coffee hangout offers a wide variety of beverages that fit into most of its customers' requests. The owner recently read an article about the benefits of healthy coffee infused with powerful nutrients. Her customers have also asked for something similar, but she is unsure of where to get a quality product her customers will enjoy. Do you have a coffee product that could meet her needs?

These are just three examples of how easy it can be to notice the businesses that operate in your area and determine if your product or service can help them increase their sales and, in turn, your retail profit and sales volume.

Another way to increase retail sales is by looking over what your customers currently purchase and suggesting a product that can help enhance what they are now buying. Some nutritional products work better when combined together. If you have a product that helps speed up metabolism, and another that is an appetite suppressant, people who are serious about controlling their weight and losing a few pounds may achieve a better result with both products rather than just one of them.

 Fact

A good salesperson knows that the more exposure a product receives, the easier it will be to sell. Many companies offer supplies such as customized stationery, business cards, Post-it notes, calendars, and refrigerator magnets with their name and logo for use in your business correspondence.

Many scented-candle companies offer attractive warmers where you can place the candle to burn safely rather than standing it alone uncovered. Your customers may be buying the candles but are unaware of the benefits of the warmer. You can easily increase your sales by displaying the advantages of the candle warmer. The only way you can do this, of course, is by discovering what your customer is already using. Then you can begin to offer suggestions for items that she could potentially be interested in.

As you offer more products they may be attracted to, don't forget to stress the many benefits your company may offer to its retail customers. Is there a solid money-back guarantee with every purchase? Are there discounts available with greater purchases? Does your company have an incentive where free products are available as a reward for consecutive monthly orders? You should be aware of any special benefits that can be gained by your customers, and make sure your customers are informed about how they work and how they can participate in the incentive.

Following Up with Retail Customers

Making just one sale should never be your intention. A good network marketer will implement some sort of system—handwritten or on your computer—that allows you to keep track of when customers need to be contacted, particularly after placing their very first order. When a customer makes an order, be sure to clarify when she should expect it to arrive and how it will get there. If it is arriving by courier service, she will most likely need to have someone at home to sign for the package.

Let her know that she should contact you once the products arrive, but don't count on that always happening. Be professional and call her when you estimate the products would have arrived. If you can go over to see her the day the products are there, that is even better, but it isn't a necessity. Use this time to make sure she's actually received what she ordered and that everything is in good condition. Sometimes during shipping and handling products may get slightly damaged, and your customer could be disappointed with the condition her order arrives in. You should also let the company know if this becomes a regular occurrence.

Once you are satisfied that the products are in good order, remind her of some of the benefits, suggest some practical ways she can use them, and be sure to leave written material that can help her understand the value of the products she has just received. If you have done your job well, you've just set up a customer that will be with you for a long time to come.

Your role now is to check in with her on a regular basis, making sure she is getting good results with what she is buying and is satisfied with how she is being treated by the company. Suggest, whenever you can, other items she may be interested in, whether for herself or people she knows that may benefit from them.

This is also a good time to find out more about her family. She may have a husband, children, and parents that would love to order the same products from you if they start to see results with your customer. Weight-loss products, skin-care products, and products that offer relief from joint pain are often the type to create immediate interest with family and friends.

Respect your customer by listening to any concerns she has or issues with the product itself. And be sure you address these issues immediately, so she has the confidence in knowing you are serious about her staying on as a regular customer.

Introducing Your Customer to New Product Releases

Your company will almost always be working to generate new, exciting products that fit into its current product line. Or it may be planning a totally new line of products that its reps have indicated they would be eager to have as part of what they can promote. Many nutritional supplement companies have also branched out into skin-care and personal-care products, and companies that have only exclusively focused on skin care have embraced the idea of adding their own range of nutritional supplements. The introduction of new products not only allows you to approach new customers that initially had no interest in your previous offer, but it also allows your current customers to have more of a choice in terms of what they can purchase.

As soon as a new product is released, it is vital that you gather as much information about it as possible to share with both your distributors and retail customers. If the product comes in a trial pack, be sure you have samples to offer. Let the customer know why the new product was introduced and the benefits it offers. If there is a special discount on the first order or an offer for ordering larger quantities, let your customers and distributors know.

Almost all new products will come with their own promotional material, which you must make sure is left with your customers to look over whether you believe they need the product or not. Let your customers know if the product may not be right for them and that you would appreciate and reward a referral if they know someone that it would appeal to. Things may change over time, and a customer may consider purchasing at a later date, or someone else may read the brochure or watch the DVD and decide to contact you and make an order.

 Essential

If the product line is new and needs explaining, make sure you invest in marketing materials in every format possible so your customers can review the information at their convenience.

Go online to see if there is promotional video you can use to help provide more buzz about your new product. Anti-aging company Jeunesse generated a lot of excitement when they used a product demonstration live on stage that helped firm the skin, particularly around the eyes, in a matter of seconds. Even before the video was turned into a promotional DVD, reps were sharing amateur footage of the product in action, and orders began rushing in months before the product was even available.

Handling Customer Service Issues

No matter how much time and effort you put in to providing exceptional customer service, there will unfortunately be occasions when something unexpectedly goes wrong. For example, a delivery gets lost, or the products arrive but half of them are missing, or you order a vanilla shake but you receive chocolate.

It helps to keep in mind that customer service issues are part and parcel of being in business, and you must learn to handle them with patience and understanding. There will be many times when the problem is something you have no control over. You may be doing everything possible to keep things flowing smoothly, then have customs officers hold your product for several days. Or the warehouse where your products are held gets flooded overnight.

You may even have situations where your customer has used the product incorrectly and developed a rash or failed to take heed of a warning on the label. The fact is, there can potentially be hundreds of issues that crop up in the world of customer service.

As a professional, you must be aware of how to handle certain situations, and be sure to involve your corporate staff and upline in any situation you feel you are unable to take care of on your own.

Here are some strategies you should apply whenever a customer service issue arises.

- **Be clear on the issue.** Ask the customer to clarify as often as needed what the problem is and what he feels needs to be done to fix it. Some issues are easily resolved and may simply be a misunderstanding.
- **Make sure you can fix it.** Not every problem can be solved by you. If the warehouse sent the wrong product or the packaging comes crushed, you can empathize with the customer's frustration, but you will need the company to help resolve the issue.
- **Don't downplay their concerns.** Your customer will often feel the issue is very important to him, no matter how trivial it may appear to you. You must stay respectful of his view of the matter and let him sincerely know it is a high priority for you.
- **Let them know what you will do next.** Are you going to e-mail the company? Will you call the company's customer service line yourself? Will you be contacting some-

one in corporate and have that person call the customer? Whatever is your next course of action, be sure to let the customer know so she is clear as to what will happen next.

- **Be prompt with any updates.** No matter what the issue, the moment you are aware of either more information or a solution, let your customer know.
- **Strive to get the best outcome.** Some issues may be easy to clear up, while others could be frustrating and complicated. Your objective is to keep the customer happy and satisfied with purchasing again through you and your company. Work through every possible way to arrive at the most convenient solution.

Every company will have a department whose role is to provide answers and support. You should utilize them at every opportunity. These representatives are trained in dealing with a variety of issues and will often have the authority to activate solutions to resolve your customer's dilemma. Be sure you use them as a resource whenever customer service issues emerge.

CHAPTER 15

Successful Online Marketing

No other technology since the audio cassette has allowed network marketing to broaden its reach as effectively as the Internet. Not only have network marketers taken to using the Internet to promote their products and opportunity; they have been at the forefront of adopting online programs and marketing software often before the mass market has even woken up to their potential.

Target the Right Market

The Internet has allowed network marketers access into a new world of possibilities. Traditional business-building methods such as contacting those in your warm market, networking with friends, or buying lead lists now have a powerful ally in the World Wide Web. The Internet allows you to determine the type of person you believe will make a positive addition to your team, and then gives you the tools and capabilities to search for prospects that fit your criteria.

Whether it is stay-at-home moms searching for extra income or professionals who are tired of working longer hours for less money, you are bound to find either an Internet forum, specialized website, or a group on a social media site such as Facebook or Instagram that caters to their concerns.

While you must be professional at all times in how you conduct yourself both online and offline, keep in mind that your activities online have even more weight to them, as pictures and words you place on the screen can easily be copied and kept as examples of the way you operate. If you join a forum and begin to come across as arrogant and pushy, it won't be long before copies of your posts are forwarded to the forum administrators and you are banned from further communications.

 Essential

Online forums can be a great way to interact with other representatives and share ideas on business building. Many also allow you to share your business website, allowing other network marketers to find out more about the company you have chosen. Just be sure to interact often with other contributors, and share your own thoughts to help create interesting conversation.

When creating a target market for your own network, the best place to begin is to search for people who have similar interests and goals as yourself. If you are big into skydiving, other people who enjoy that activity will be more open to listening to why a fellow skydiver has looked at ways to build a business where he can free up more time. If you place great value on totally natural skin care, your products will more likely appeal to people who also see that as important and can sincerely see you are passionate about that interest.

This idea applies to almost anything you have a personal interest in. Your hobbies and other leisure activities can provide you with an excellent first foot in the door by helping create rapport with your target market. From there, you can begin to scout for groups where particular skills and characteristics are vital to forming a strong organization. Those involved in sales, public speaking, and personal development classes make great potential team members. Coaches, teachers, and trainers are excellent prospects to consider, as their skills in teaching and mentoring are huge assets to your business.

Be proactive and write out exactly the type of person you are looking to partner with. Be very clear regarding the skills and characteristics you are considering. If you choose, you can refine this description to include the age group, location, and other categories that can help identify the right candidate.

From there, get to work and ask your immediate network if they know people that fit your criteria and look online for avenues to promote your search for the right team members to join your business.

Develop an Online Marketing Plan

With so many options cropping up daily, it takes a lot of preparation when it comes to creating a plan for your online marketing. What you do online plays a significant role in building your business, but if you don't work off a plan, you can easily find yourself immersed in a lot of time-wasting activities.

The best way to do this is to first develop a list of the types of online marketing options you have decided to focus on. Include social media sites and applications such as Pinterest and Facebook, plus websites you have either developed yourself or are using through your company, such as a replicated prospecting site. If you are thinking of starting a blog, also be sure to create fresh content and maintain the blog with updates.

You will then need to work out the most effective way to stay on top of every approach. Online marketing works well when you consistently utilize a tactic. Try to post to Facebook two times a day and stick to that schedule as close as you can. If you update your blog once a week, stay steady with that number.

Think about your other commitments during the day, and try to carve out a period of time you will commit to online marketing. If you decide to just do it when you get free time, it's not going to happen. You are bound to get caught up doing other things that are unrelated to your business.

You will need at least twenty or thirty minutes daily to invest in your online marketing. If you are writing blog posts and getting involved in online forums, that can easily spread to an hour a day.

 **Essential**

Many prospects will do a quick search online to find information about the business in your country. Setting up a blog that promotes company information and has details about you will help promote you as a leader in your market. Make sure you leave easy to find contact details with a well thought out profile and professional picture.

Once you have refined the approaches you will use and developed a workable time schedule, get to work in creating a personal brand online that reflects both yourself and your company. A combination of well-written posts, images that appeal to your target market, and even videos of you sharing a message are what works best.

Whenever possible with your online marketing, use hashtags with words that appeal to those who are following your posts. If you post something about your new weight-loss product, hashtagging could look like this: "All-new, natural weight-loss product has helped like no other product. My friends are winning too . . . take a look at this pic of Julie! #natural #health #weightloss #slim." Placing the hashtag in front of key words will help highlight those words online and allow interested followers of those subjects find you a lot easier.

Another key part to your online plan is to be sure every form of marketing you use interacts with whatever else you are utilizing. So if you are using Instagram, the website you promote with your posts should lead back to your own site. Your blog should include online buttons that allow your readers to follow you through your links on social media. Your Facebook posts every now and then should remind your friends that you also post interesting information on

Twitter. And your profile description on everything should provide a link for any form of online marketing you can be found on.

 Alert

An intention to spend just a few minutes a day on the Internet can easily turn into hours of unproductive activity. It takes a lot of discipline to not get sucked into the whirlpool of online distractions, but you must stay focused.

Remember, online marketing is still about having people know you, like you, and trust you. It's been referred to as relationship marketing on steroids. Once you have those three musts in order, the chances of prospects being open to hearing your marketing messages are increased. Be consistent, stay professional, and work toward building a following of people who enjoy your output and your interaction.

Should You Have a Website?

A common question asked by many new people to the industry is whether they need their own personalized website in order to start their business properly. Perhaps the question that you really need to ask is: What will you use the website for? Is it to promote your opportunity or product? Will you be selling your products through your site?

The idea that you can put together a great site and sponsor people with ease is simply not practical. Remember that websites don't sponsor people—people sponsor people. No matter how good the information on your site is, if the basic trust and confidence in you and what you represent is not there, people may love what they see on your site but still choose not to participate.

A common danger in using personalized websites is that if you create one that works really well, your new team members will feel that they will need a similar type of site. If you have spent a small fortune setting yours up, and your new team member doesn't have the budget to do the same, he may feel that the website will become the missing link in his business-building efforts.

 Alert

If you choose to create your own site, make sure you run it by your company's legal department and marketing team. You don't want the site to be taken down after thousands of dollars have been spent getting it together.

Network marketing trainer Randy Gage is credited with saying, "It doesn't matter if it works, it only matters that it duplicates." What this means is that those things you apply in your business that cannot be duplicated by the majority of your team will prove to be a sticking point down the road. If it's a website that works really well for you but the majority of your team cannot do the same, you risk this becoming an issue as your business expands.

The other thing you can look to for consistency and stronger duplication is your company's replicated site. This site can be used by anybody that is a team member, is obtainable for a small monthly investment, and is created by your company's marketing department so it complies with company guidelines. Most replicated sites are also a "squeeze page," which means they include the option for people who come across your site to offer their e-mail address for potential contact in the future.

Blogging

A weblog, or blog, is the term used to describe an online journal. Available in a variety of formats, blogs are used by millions of people around the world to detail their thoughts and interests so they can share them with anybody who may be interested. Most blogs offer some form of interaction with the blog writer, which then allows the blogger to get feedback and support in relation to her posts.

The key to blogging is consistency. People love to read blogs that are current and updated regularly. Blogs that cover a niche section of society or are mildly controversial are the most popular. People are fascinated in reading the thoughts and ideas of writers who do not form a part of the mainstream media. Blogging gives them a voice and a platform.

There are dozens of websites where you can begin a blog, many at no cost to the user. Try Google's Blogger at *http://blogger.com*, Squarespace at *www.squarespace.com*, or the WordPress platform at *https://wordpress.com*. Don't use your blog as just a selling tool. Think of it as a way to share your thoughts on what is happening in your business and your life. Use plenty of images and honest feedback in your writing while relating the ups and downs of growing a business. Your readers want to feel you're a real person, not an advertising tool. Blogs can be a lot of fun and extremely rewarding when done correctly. They do, however, require you to be creative and open to interaction. Read a few blogs first before setting one up yourself to determine if it is something you would like to focus on.

Videos

Online videos are a very powerful way to share the benefits of not only your business but also you and your team members. People love to see and hear what you stand for. Videos give you the opportunity to show the real you, rather than having prospects just reading what you have to say or viewing a still image.

Don't think that your videos need to be of high quality, filmed in a studio with a green screen in the background. Marketers that are succeeding with videos are simply taking out their smartphone, clicking "record," and then sharing their thoughts as they kick back on the beach or excitedly walk out of their company's convention.

Your prospects aren't sitting back analyzing your lighting and camera work. Social media has adjusted our expectations. Your prospects aren't looking for perfection; they're looking for something that is genuine. The more real, sincere, and approachable you appear, the more likely they will feel they can talk to you about what you do. Facebook, Google+, and the Periscope application allow you to film videos on the spot and post them online in minutes. With millions of eyes glued to screens all over the world, just getting thirty or forty people you have never met to view your video and gain an insight into who you are and what you do is a terrific result that can have a great effect on your business.

Online Advertising

With over a billion people at any one time online surfing the Internet, it only makes sense that network marketers would also eventually consider advertising online to attract more people to their network and products. Online advertising can definitely get you a wider audience, but it can also turn into a money drain if not handled correctly.

Facebook and Google lead the field when it comes to pay-per-click advertising. With this method, you pick a key word or words that someone might search for, then create a small classified ad and attach a link. Whenever anybody searches for your word or words, your ad appears on the page. And if someone clicks on your link, you will be charged a small fee from a few pennies to several dollars and even higher, depending on how much you (and others who might be trying to buy ads for the same search terms) are willing to pay. This has been proven as a viable method in creating website traffic for many network marketers, and in its early days, Google—through its AdWords program—was seen as the must-use strategy for network marketers embracing the Internet.

While almost all Internet browsers offer similar advertising methods, Google remains the most popular and most effective. In 2007, Facebook was looking for ways to increase its immense reach into the daily lives of its users and began to allow its business users to place advertising in users' feeds for a fee. In 2009, Facebook basically adopted a similar approach as Google AdWords and allowed all users to create classified ads that appealed to those on Facebook with targeted interests. Facebook upped the ante in early 2012 when Sponsored Story was introduced, allowing marketers to have their message appear in your News Feed, directed at your interests. Twitter had introduced a similar system months earlier, which only confirmed that marketers were open to this form of advertising.

Banner advertising on websites is still popular, but you would need to weigh whether the costs are worth the results. Many marketers have found banner advertising not that effective at promoting business opportunities. One strategy you can apply when it comes to banner advertising is to think about it purely for product sales rather than attracting new business builders. You can have the banners appear on sites where users may have an interest in your product based on the site they're on or even in relation to search words they have entered into a browser.

Selling your product through Craigslist and eBay can also be used to promote your goods, but be aware that customers who are searching through these sites are looking for discounted products and trying to find a bargain. If you are selling high-quality nutritional products or a very exclusive skin-care range, your results through many of these online markets may not be what you are looking for. Also keep in mind that many companies do not allow this type of selling, as it may tarnish the company's brand and diminish the value of its products.

Easily being found online, or search engine optimization (SEO), is another powerful form of advertising, and there isn't a high cost for this. A popular blog, a website with a high traffic count, and regular posting to social media sites are ways you can have your material easily found by those searching for key words related to your business.

E-Newsletters

An electronic form of a physical newsletter, e-newsletters are an effective way to communicate with both your team members and prospects. Many leaders in the industry will use a different newsletter to cover both sections of people, with many stories crossing over into both newsletters.

People love to read about great product results, a successful new team member who has been promoted quickly, or a company promotion that they believe they can win. Make your newsletter colorful, with plenty of images and stories. Keep the wording brief, as many readers will be reading off a screen and will tend to scan rather than spend extra minutes reading a detailed story.

 Fact

According to eMarketer, in 2015 there are 156 million tablets being used in the United States, with worldwide usage topping over 1 billion. This makes it even more crucial that the tools you use can adapt to the tablet format. This also applies to presentations on smartphones, allowing your prospect to view your message as rapidly as possible.

In newsletters to prospects, stay clear of using jargon and technical talk that may confuse them and have them lose interest. Remember, you're still working to get them interested in either trying your products or joining your business. If it sounds too difficult, prospects will put off making a decision.

Newsletters to your team should feature product testimonials, success stories, and regular tips on how to better use the products or build the business. Try to use exciting subject lines in your e-mail when the newsletter is sent out. "Newsletter No.193" is bland compared to "From Zero to Hero! Find out How Ziggy McLaine Achieved Diamond in Six Months!" as your subject line.

Finally, be sure to include a call to action with every copy. Is it to order a new product? Register for the next event? Submit a testimonial on a recently released product? Whatever it is, be clear about what you want your readers to take action on. There are several excellent providers of software, such as Constant Contact (*www.constantcontact.com*) and Swiftpage (*www.swiftpage.com*), that allow you to create your own e-newsletters. Many others can be found by typing "e-newsletter software" into your browser's search bar.

Creating Successful E-Mails

From the day the Internet landed on our computer screens, the ability to write to each other online rapidly turned into a standard form of communication. Over 100 billion e-mails a day are sent all over the globe, and you can be sure that messages and promotions from network marketers make up a good portion of them.

It's important you make sure your e-mails are written to reflect the brand that you have cultivated through social media and in person. One shoddy e-mail filled with misspellings or poor grammar could leave your prospect or new team member with lingering questions regarding your professionalism.

 Alert

Sending unsolicited e-mail, known as "spamming," is not only annoying—it's illegal. Only send personalized e-mail messages to people who have shown some interest in your products or business.

E-mail campaigns to your prospects should be handled differently than those to team members, which should be used to communicate what is happening with your team and company. A call to action should always be present, and just as importantly, the option to stop the e-mails should be available to anyone receiving your e-mails. It also goes without saying that you should include all possible ways to contact you in case your prospect has a question or feedback.

Here are just a few tips on creating e-mails that will increase their effectiveness:

- **Have an interesting subject line.** Your reader will look at the subject line to determine if she should open the e-mail now or later. A hypey subject line will often be ignored, or the message won't be taken seriously. A boring, nondescript subject line creates no interest for the reader. Subject lines that ask a question, mention a first name, or include a personal fact will improve the chances of your e-mail being read immediately.
- **Be sure to use CC and BCC properly.** We've all seen it happen—the carbon copy (CC) box is filled with e-mail addresses that should have been kept private by using blind carbon copy (BCC). Unless you are 100 percent sure you want everyone to see who else is on this e-mail thread, keep multiple receivers in the BCC box.
- **Keep it brief.** Readers tend to scan e-mail first, and may go back to your message and read it in depth later if they deem it important. Stick with a brief message and you have a greater chance that your e-mail is not placed in the "read it later" category.
- **Check for spelling and grammar.** Your spell checker should be operating at all times when writing for business, but it also pays to read through your e-mail prior to sending to make sure nothing has been missed.

- **Don't include emoticons.** The smiley faces and thumbs-up signs are okay when dealing with personal matters and close friends. But the accountant who is looking at your business trying to see if you would make the right partner will probably wonder why you use the same symbols that his sixteen-year-old sends out.
- **Never use all capitals.** An e-mail with all caps gives the impression you are shouting, and you could be perceived as someone who is new to using a keyboard.
- **Greet the reader.** You don't need to be overly formal, but you do need to acknowledge the recipient by addressing his or her first name. Don't start any e-mail by getting straight into your message without recognizing the reader.
- **End the e-mail appropriately.** Sign off with a "Kind regards" or something of that nature. If your e-mail is part of a longer thread, say six or seven e-mails after each other, it will allow the reader to quickly work out where each of your messages has finished.

The Importance of Responding

One of the most common frustrations your customers and even team members will share is how often the leader they have tried to contact is either extremely slow to respond or is unreachable. If you have been sent an e-mail and you fail to respond within at least forty-eight hours, you can be sure that the person who has contacted you feels that she is not important to you. That's just human nature. You can overcome that by making sure you respond to messages as early as you can, even if it's a "Can I get back to you later?" reply. When you do eventually respond, be sure you have read and understood the initial inquiry, and then reply in a manner that allows the recipient to feel his message was important to you.

Online Writing Tips

While most writers think that there is no difference between writing online and writing in a physical format, you should be aware of several distinctions between the two. Online writing has to be different due to the nature of reading on a screen. Online readers are scanners rather than in-depth readers, and they search for highlights or bullet points in order to move on as quickly as possible. They're essentially rushing through their information because they have very limited time with an even shorter attention span.

 Essential

Do not photocopy or reuse company-owned images from the Internet unless you have permission to do so from the company. You could be violating several different laws including trademarks and copyrights.

These are the things you have to keep in mind when writing copy for the Internet:

- Good, descriptive headlines are vital, as they will lead the reader to what he may view as important to scan through.
- Use shorter words online so the reader doesn't have to pause to think of what the words mean. "Prerogative" means the same thing as "choice;" however, one is easier to understand while skimming a page than the other.
- Try to keep your facts to the point, and avoid confusion in how they can be understood. You don't want your reader going back over a sentence four of five times in order to get your point.
- Use stories as often as possible. People enjoy stories, and they are a great way to get a message through. If it's a

story of someone they know either personally or publicly, even better. If they can visualize the person you're telling the story about, it will make a stronger impression in their mind.

- Last but not least, try to stay clear of words that are only a part of your business but make no sense to those outside of it. This isn't always easy when you are writing how-to information for your business and there aren't other words or labels to use as a description, but you should do your best to at least add in a simple explanation that translates your jargon to the reader who has come across your site for the first time.

CHAPTER 16

The Power of Social Media

What was initially branded Internet 2.0 rapidly transformed into what is known today as social media. It is embedded into our everyday lives, altering everything from the way we view our society to the way we view ourselves. In an age where promotional messages must be whittled down to 140 characters, and the success of advertising campaigns is measured by the "Likes" on a post, network marketers have adopted social media as a powerful voice in cutting through the marketing maze.

The New World of Social Marketing

It would be difficult to come across anybody in today's world that is not somehow accessing some form of social media on the Internet. Whether it's a YouTube video, a blog post, or a Twitter feed, our world revolves around the views, news, and reviews that can be posted by anybody, from butchers in Birmingham to barbers in Beirut.

Social media has leveled the playing field and given everyone a place to voice an opinion. It allows you to air your concerns while you sit in your bedroom in Dallas, Texas, and receive advice just minutes later from someone you have never met in, say, Dubai, United Arab Emirates.

Network marketers have embraced the social media scene, utilizing every avenue possible to create awareness of their products, promote their opportunity, and brand themselves as successful professionals in the world of network marketing. Many marketers have worked the social media scene exceptionally well, while others seem unsure of how to utilize Facebook, LinkedIn, Twitter, and other available formats to professionally and effectively promote their business. While they can see the benefits of having a whole new universe of prospects to connect with, they may often promote their business in ways that produce next to no results or, worse, offend those they interact with.

 Essential

Try to support other network marketers you see building a business on social media. As they learn to trust and know you, you stand a better chance of them being open to hearing about your business in the future. This also might deflect any criticism from you if something goes bad with the company you rep and helps to continue to promote network marketing as a professional business.

For the most part, social media is a fun way to share with friends and family what you've been up to and what is happening in your life. It also gives you a convenient way to follow their life events without them having to pick up the phone or write a detailed letter relating the latest events in their lives. Convenience of use and the speed at which these updates can be shared has been a prime reason behind social media's enormous growth, as well as fueling the growth of the network marketing industry.

There are some people who fear using social media sites, worried that their personal privacy is there for all to uncover. While many of those fears may have had some truth to them in the early days, almost all social media sites now have a variety of preferences to help safeguard whom you choose to interact with and how much information can be viewed by others. Control over what you share and with whom you share it is in your hands, and staying safe on the Internet using these sites has drastically improved.

Of course, it pays to use common sense. Posting photos you would not want your grandmother seeing is probably something you should think twice about. If you have to think for thirty seconds about whether something you are about to put up on a site is appropriate or not, then take it as a no. Just remember, information you place on the net can be downloaded or copied in seconds. By the time you hurriedly delete a picture or video that you accidently posted, your best friends may have it on their hard drives ready to e-mail to their college buddies! It doesn't mean you need to be afraid of using the Internet and social media sites; it just requires you apply sound judgment when placing anything on the Internet open for public viewing.

What confuses many entering the world of social media marketing is the multitude of options now available to anybody who wants to get involved in marketing through this format. While Facebook and Twitter are considered the biggest players in town, there are other sites that offer benefits you should consider.

Facebook

When Mark Zuckerberg, Eduardo Saverin, and several of their college roommates developed thefacebook.com in early 2004, the idea was to help college and university students by allowing them to list personal achievements and attributes alongside their picture. Facebook has now developed into a web portal that services over 1.5 billion active monthly users. Since 2006, anyone who is at least thirteen years old has been permitted to become a registered user, and experts estimate that one in every eleven people in the world has taken that option.

There is no cost to register with Facebook, and creating a user profile simply requires you have an e-mail address. Once you are registered, you are guided through creating your user profile and page, and then you are free to begin adding friends.

Your News Feed, which is essentially a wall you can scroll through to see what everyone else is posting, is used to place written messages, share videos, and post pictures. Without going into every detail about how to use Facebook, suffice to say the layout is very easy to follow and apply.

 Fact

Despite its humble beginnings, the owners of Facebook were offered $10 million in 2004 by two different investors. They flatly turned them both down.

Facebook offers you the advantage of creating private groups, where you can teach and train your team, and public groups that relate to your personal interests. The site also offers a private message service that allows you to interact with other users without having to write anything directly on their wall. In regards to creating friendships and developing new connections, Facebook seems the most user-friendly. The site also allows for advertising messages by users on a pay-per-click basis.

Twitter

Twitter is a site that allows users to post short messages, called Tweets, capped at 140 characters. Launched in March 2006, there are now over 300 million users of the service, many preferring the briefer, more pointed format over other platforms.

Twitter users interact by posting their own thoughts, sharing the views of others by Re-tweeting something they liked and want others to read, or by clicking the "favorite" star, which alerts the writer that you enjoyed his or her post. Direct messages, which allow you to contact other users privately, are also possible within Twitter.

🛑 Alert

Social media has allowed everyone a new level of transparency. If you are doing anything unethical or without integrity, you can be sure the word will slowly filter through the social media grapevine. Something you may have done several years ago can quickly come back into the spotlight, so be sure you are acting in line with the image you want to portray on social media.

Twitter accounts are also free, and once you are registered, setting up your profile is easy. Be sure to use a picture of yourself and not your company's logo or a picture of your product. People want to know about you and your interests. They want to interact with a real person.

Once you are set up you will receive a Twitter "handle," which is the "at" symbol (@) followed by your chosen user name. Other users will then be able to interact with you by using your Twitter handle. Twitter is a place where wit and wisdom works best, so be sure your profile description reflects your fun side as well as any unique aspects about your personality.

Instagram

If you believe that a picture speaks a thousand words, Instagram may be more up your alley. This service allows you to take pictures and short videos and post them to your Instagram timeline, which can be viewed by followers of your account.

Setting up an account is extremely simple and free. As the site is now owned by Facebook, you can even use your Facebook login details to start an account with Instagram. Your uploaded photos can be shared on Facebook, Twitter, and Tumblr directly from Instagram, giving you a greater audience. A clever aspect of the site is the ability to filter your photos in order to enhance an image or give it a quirky look.

Don't want everyone to view your pictures? No problem. Instagram allows you to shift to a private setting, allowing only registered followers to view your posted pictures.

Pinterest

How many times have you found yourself browsing the Internet, seen something you would like to check out later, but wish there was somewhere you could pin it first? Well, that is exactly what you have with Pinterest. This unique application has been used for everything from creating an inspiration board to keeping track of the latest trends related to your interests.

You can sign in with your Facebook login, or create new account details just for Pinterest. Once you're registered, you can begin to view other users' public Pinterest boards, which are often grouped into categories, some inspiring, many unusual, all interesting. You'll also receive the Pinterest virtual pin, which is added to your browser and can be clicked whenever you see a picture or article you want to pin to your board.

Pinterest also includes a helpful feature where followers who click on your pictures are taken to the site they were pinned from. For networkers who maintain a blog or their own website, this is extremely useful in getting interested prospects to eventually view your marketing message.

LinkedIn

LinkedIn is the world's largest online business network, boasting over 260 million members in over 200 countries, and a further two new members joining every second.

While many people may not view LinkedIn the way they view Facebook or Twitter in terms of interaction, the website does allow for professional promotion of your business and your identity in relation to what you specialize in. Based around the philosophy of creating stronger networks in order to create better professional opportunities, LinkedIn can help you stay in touch with business owners and authorities from all over the globe who can potentially put you in touch with exactly the type of person you may be looking for.

While LinkedIn has traditionally been used for those looking to find work in areas where they may have previously had no connections, the format is now just as powerful in sharing information regarding your business that may interest followers of your profile.

Google+

Google's answer to the Facebook phenomenon, Google+ was launched in 2011 as an alternative for social media users who wanted more out of their online experience. Integration with other Google applications such as YouTube and Gmail, plus a preference by the Google browser to raise the ranking of Google+ posts with search results, helped create a strong early fan base. Many users enjoy using Google+ due to the belief that the interaction on the site is more genuine than the more fickle nature of Facebook users. Members claim that users of Google+ are more serious about participating in conversations and reading posts that may otherwise go unnoticed on Facebook. Similar to Facebook, Google+ works by having members share their thoughts, pictures, and videos onto a stream where they can also control who views the post based on a system called Circles. Your personal friends can be placed in one circle, and business contacts can be placed in another. You may then share on Google+ and control who gets to see which message.

In May 2013, Google integrated its Hangouts app, a group chat video feature that allows live visual streaming and interaction.

YouTube

Another popular social media site that sits in the Google stable, YouTube is the world's most popular video sharing site with over a billion users. Visitors may view and share any video on the site that is public, and can upload their own videos by becoming a member. While the idea for YouTube came about when a market for amateur footage of world events emerged, much of what is on the site today is an entertaining mix of family videos filmed on a smartphone and mainstream channels creating their own online network.

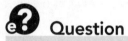 **Question**

What's the maximum length for a video on YouTube?
The default limit for all users is fifteen minutes; however, accounts that are in good standing and can be verified by phone can seek an extension of over two hours.

Network marketers have utilized YouTube to promote both their products and opportunity. Short videos highlighting special events work extremely well, with many companies now using YouTube to draw attention to their annual convention or to promote a new product or distributor incentive. YouTube's popularity has increased due to its ease of use and its unending new material that caters to any interest.

Periscope

Launched by Twitter in March 2015, Periscope is a live video-streaming application that allows you to film through your smartphone and have users view your video as you film. You may then post the video to Twitter, controlling the privacy of who can and cannot view it. Although still in its infancy, the idea behind Periscope is intriguing. The opportunity to view any event as it happens live simply by looking through the lens of another phone is both exciting and fascinating.

Network marketers are now beginning to see the opportunities with Periscope, using it to live-stream special events and home meetings and to invite team members to join them at exclusive gatherings to help motivate those that could not be there.

An Effective Social Media Plan

You now have a good insight into the many options available in the world of social media. It should be noted there are many more sites and applications to choose from, and you could easily be online all day and night searching for every possible site that caters to your tastes. Your goal is to find the ones that are most suitable and use them effectively in order to achieve the results you are looking for.

But what are the rules when it comes to network marketers? What can you do to stay professional, not be frowned upon by your Facebook friends, and keep up your image as a successful, professional network marketer? Let's first stick to two vital principles that will apply to everything you do on social media sites.

 Alert

Social media is wonderful, but it can also become a huge distraction and waste a lot of your time. Spending hours watching online videos and reading up on posts from Facebook are great when you are done with business matters, but it will hurt you if you let social media take up most of your producing hours.

Number one: people join your business when they know you, like you, and trust you. This applies both online and offline, but it needs a lot more work online since you are meeting many prospects for the first time. Remember, whether online or offline, it is still about building relationships.

Number two: promote, don't prospect. This slight difference in the way you approach your social media makes a huge difference in how you come across to others. With that said, let's look at how you can use the power of social media in relation to your network-marketing business. Here is a quick analogy of how not to do it. For a moment, imagine this scenario . . .

You walk into a party held in a huge hall in your city. There are dozens of people here you know very well and many close friends that you see regularly. There are also many of your family members whose company you really enjoy. Mixed among the crowd are over 200 partygoers that you've never met before. Some seem friendly and approachable; others may not even notice you at all, and you're okay with that. For tonight though, you're all together at one great party, having a good time and socializing and getting to know each other.

While everyone is talking and laughing, you hear many interesting things, a lot of funny discussions, and some people that sound just plain dull. You arrived with the idea of promoting your business (not what parties are for!), but you're not quite sure how to go about it. So unfortunately, you do what untrained amateurs do, which is walk around slamming everyone with your opportunity.

"Hey Jane, get into my business now and you can be in Hawaii this January! Take my card and call me first thing in the morning to get started!"

"Andrew, buddy, aren't you sick of your job? Come to this meeting on Tuesday night and you can sack your boss by Thursday, trust me!"

"Hey everyone, look at me and listen! I have a home business where you can make ten grand a month in six months minimum, e-mail me for details; I'm going to pass everyone a card right now!"

It sounds crude, right? How long would people want you at a social occasion like this with you walking around putting this message out? Everyone would pretty quickly work out who to avoid and, worse, who to never invite again! Yet, this is very similar to what many networkers do today on Facebook, Twitter, and other social media sites. They join the party while everyone is having a good time, then contribute nothing but repeated hype about their incredible business and amazing product. People soon get weary of their constant requests for people to join their business. They either ignore them or unfriend them, adding to a growing list of those who take a dim view of how network marketer's operate their businesses.

As a network marketer, you don't want to appear like this. You want to stay professional and have people feel you are the right type of person to partner with. Remember: promote, don't prospect. This means that you let people know what is happening with your life and business without hounding them to constantly join you or buy something. You can hint to those who follow you on social media as to what you are doing and where you may be travelling thanks to your network marketing business, just don't blatantly prospect people.

So how do you take this instruction and implement it via social media? It's a lot easier than you may think. Social media has allowed us to connect with more people than ever before. Some argue that's it not a real connection and many aren't real friends, just faces on a screen who write back every now and then. That's true to a point, but we must take into account that real people with real human wants and needs sit behind the other side of the screen you're looking at.

Many of these people, properly approached, are willing to look at what you have to offer with your business if they are also interested in a better lifestyle, greater income, and increased opportunity to travel. So get them to know you, earn their trust, and do the right thing when they put their hand up to find out more about what you do.

When you start to develop an online rapport with people, take notice of what is happening in their lives. Leave comments every now and then, and click the like, favorite, or +1 button on your site if you see something you honestly do like. (Don't "like" everything; that's a sure-fire way of saying, "I'm not reading anything; I'm on autopilot.")

The key here is that they will eventually notice you and take an interest in your updates too. And remember, you're not aiming to sledgehammer them with your business; you just want them to notice the good things happening with it—things they may be interested in and would like to know more about.

 Essential

Pictures and video will usually draw more attention than a written post. Your social media efforts are competing with posts from hundreds of other users on the average user's News Feed. Use attractive, interesting images to stand out in the crowd.

Are you going on an overseas trip for your business? Write about it and post some exciting pictures. Have you lost weight with your products? Put up an online testimonial. Have you received a saving or credit on your energy bill? Post a copy of the bill. Pictures speak. Are you having dinner with your team at a top restaurant in town? Then post the pictures. Let people see what type of business you have and how it helps your life and, in turn, can help theirs. People will want to find out more, and these types of shares open the door for you to tell them more.

The essential tactic is to then take the business talk with your prospect off the social media landscape as fast you can and begin a discussion with them in the real world. Get onto Skype, send an e-mail, or agree to get on the phone. Just work to take the rest of your follow-up with prospects into an environment where they can see you eye to eye and can shake your hand. Remember, you want to show them you're a real person, just like them. Let them hear your voice and realize they can trust you and you are willing to help them. This is vital!

Pay close attention to what it is they are looking for and provide the information they are requesting. Not all your prospecting tools will be applicable to each prospect; that's why you need to ask questions about what you can do to help them. The better you listen and focus on them, the more likely they will feel they can trust you.

As with most things, developing a smooth routine in order for this to be done right takes time and practice. Like developing relationships and prospecting in other ways, you will need to develop the skills and get into a groove with this as well. Just work on it, stay active, do the right thing in a professional manner, and before long you will find that using social media to help grow your contact base is an enjoyable and effective part of building your business.

Checklist: Succeeding with Social Media

Using social media to grow your business can be a lot of fun, but there are also many pitfalls. To make it work for your business, here are some easy to follow pointers on what to avoid and what to focus on.

- ❐ Share highlights of your personal life, allowing followers to see you as a real person living a fun, high-quality life.
- ❐ Be approachable. Be sure to include a professional profile picture of yourself, and be open and prompt in replying to private messages.
- ❐ Don't spam groups with your opportunity. This is the quickest way to get banned on most groups and could also land you in trouble with some social media sites. Facebook is known to suspend accounts when users have abused its agreement.

- ☐ Use social media to develop relationships with people you would not have the chance to meet face-to-face in your normal daily life. Remember that people will only join you if they know you, like you, and trust you.
- ☐ Use hashtags whenever possible. This will allow you to highlight the words that could appeal to your target market and allow prospects to easily find you and what you promote.
- ☐ Be consistent. No matter how often you post or where you do it, stay disciplined enough to stick with the pattern you set. Your followers will soon learn to expect when you are active and where to find you.
- ☐ Take the relationship offline once you have developed trust online. The moment your prospect has made it clear she wants to find out more about you and your products, suggest someplace where you can meet face-to-face.

There's nothing on this list that can't be perfected with a bit of time and practice. Building a business and meeting new people through social media is not the only way, but it definitely should be something you look into and learn to do well.

CHAPTER 17

Learn as You Earn

There are no formal degrees or diplomas required for you to succeed in network marketing. This business allows you to gain experience while developing your income. While many professions require you to spend years in learning mode, investing thousands of dollars before you can even apply that education, your school in network marketing is the real world. It doesn't matter what your level of education is; as long as you are willing to get into action and learn along the way, you can succeed in this business.

Product Training

No matter what your product line is—from electricity to energy drinks—you absolutely must know about it, why it works, and which part of the market would find it most appealing.

The first place you should look is your company's website. Most companies' websites will have a section that provides information about their product range, the story of how they were discovered or invented, and even testimonials of results. You should use these testimonials to gain an insight into how other customers are using the product and also to share with potential customers that you have.

A product catalog is next on the list of what you should look for. Catalogs will usually list every product available, what each product is for, and how to use it. A price for every product may or may not be listed, but you can keep a separate price list in case your company hasn't provided one.

 Alert

Your company will also provide product training at most of its events. You may be able to attend a doctors' forum if you are involved with nutrition, or your company may call in a consultant in the industry that specializes in your service.

The Internet is a great place to research helpful information. If your product contains the antioxidant glutathione, you will probably be hard-pressed to find customers and new reps who readily understand what glutathione is and why your body needs it. In fact, they may also be unaware of the benefits of antioxidants.

This is where a bit of online reading can come in handy, because you can access analyses published by doctors and researchers that could help you gain a better understanding of the science behind ingredients than even your company has provided. While it is important you know and understand your product's benefits, be careful of slowly turning in to the product "expert." This happens when reps start to believe they have to know everything about everything when it comes to their product line. This is simply not the case.

Remember, you're the messenger, not the message. Your role is to put the information in people's hands and allow them to do the research themselves. If you sit there for an hour drilling your customer on how electricity is generated, why your super juice has a 3 percent higher ORAC score, or why the apples your company uses are sliced in the Netherlands then stored in oak barrels for eight weeks, your customer will switch off, get a glazed look in his eyes, and politely let you know he doesn't think it's for him.

 Alert

Be very careful about making product claims that are not verified by your company first. If regulators catch on to something you have printed or verbally claimed that cannot be proven, you will land both your company and yourself in a lot of trouble.

Product training also entails learning more about your company. How was it founded? What is its history? What are its best-selling items? Why does it sell through the direct-sales/network marketing format? These kinds of questions relate to product training for two reasons. First, when people purchase your products, they are also buying the brand name, so you want to know what stands behind that name. Second, the company's reputation in relation to its products is a major selling point when it comes to discussing your business with prospects.

Sales Training

Your sales training is based on two major selling points:

1. Selling your product or service to customers both in an out of your network.
2. Selling your business opportunity to prospects interested in developing a second income and a part-time, home-based business.

In order to succeed in network marketing, you must learn how to present both, and do so in a manner that others can see themselves comfortably doing. This is why traditional sales strategies have not worked as well in network marketing. While some form of answering objections and closing a sale are required, many of the older techniques to get your prospect to sign on the dotted line have not crossed over so well into the world of network marketing.

Today's network marketers take a more consultative approach when it comes to sharing both their business and products. And companies have adjusted their training in terms of product sales and new team member recruiting to reflect this shift. Your sales training is now more likely to cover how to share benefits and features, how to locate the best prospects, and the proper way of inviting. Then, the focus will be on learning the desires of the prospect, how to be aware of the prospect's needs when researching the company, and why a prospect is even looking to get involved.

 Essential

Your job is not to convince or coerce anybody. Your job is to provide enough information so your prospect can make her own educated decision about what she would like to do. You're searching for the people who are looking for what you provide, as they will be most likely to be ready for your message.

This means that rather than focusing on getting someone to sign on at any cost, your sales training should focus on creating rapport, listening techniques, and providing your prospect with the information necessary so he can make his own decision in his own time.

Your company, upline, and even generic network marketing training events will provide all the training you need in learning to excel in this area. The reps who talk to more people have more people come into their business. It is all numbers. If a rep only talks to one person a month, then it could be months before someone comes into her business. In other words, the reps who show their plan or product the most win. Training events, online videos, webinars, and conference calls are all educational tools you can use to learn the correct and most effective sales strategies.

Company Events

If there is a shortcut in building a network-marketing business, it's to get yourself and your team to your company events. Time and time again, major events have proven to be the most powerful way to motivate reps and inspire them to grow their business. Events develop belief and confidence. They help instill courage in even the most uncertain team member.

Major events will often feature guest speakers and leaders in the company who have made incredible progress. Some companies will even regularly host politicians, guest speakers, and media celebrities. Events aren't only about learning the nuts and bolts of how to build a business; they are a great way to connect with new friends and leaders in your company. Many times, what is overheard in the halls or traveling down an escalator can be the very thing you needed to hear. It may be the spark you needed to get your belief back.

The industry is filled with story after story of reps who have come close to quitting or felt frustrated to the point of despair who then attended an event where something that was said or a private conversation with a leader has transformed their whole life. Many events feature recognition of top achievers, plus a short speech from those who have reached significant levels in the compensation plan. Just one story, or even a sentence, from what is said from the stage could be enough to propel you or a leader in your team to reach higher levels in your company.

There are various forms of events held by companies, but almost every company will hold an annual convention, which is the highlight event for all reps to attend. It is often at a convention where new products are released and major company announcements are made. Smaller regional events can be very powerful, as they can provide your team more of an opportunity to meet guest speakers and mingle with other reps who live in their vicinity.

Conferences for women, no matter the product or service, are gaining momentum. Women, for the most part, are very relational and tend to train differently than men. This is not to say either training is better than the other; it is just different. So women should take advantage of these conferences when available, and men should encourage the women on their team to participate. It will be beneficial for all parties.

Also, top leaders in a company will hold a weekly or monthly business presentation in which reps are encouraged to attend and bring along their prospects who are interested in finding out more about the business in a formal setting.

You must take advantage of every event to help strengthen your belief in your venture and help educate yourself in all aspects of building your business. This means learning about the products, how to promote your business, and how to develop your personal skills so you become a more attractive business partner. An event allows you the opportunity to hear from those with many years of experience and to receive an education directly from those who have succeeded at network marketing—all in a short amount of time.

As you continue to grow your business and meet leaders within your company, you will also discover that every single leader will absolutely tell you that regular attendance of all events played a significant role in his or her success, and that success would have never been achieved without the events being there to support his or her team.

Keep in mind that your company event may not only appeal to those already in the business. Your prospects may be interested in attending your product training, or even your regional or national conventions. These prospects are looking to get a greater insight into how the business works, the training involved, and the culture of your team and company. Whatever the reason is, whether it is a rep or prospect, make sure you are constantly working to have people experience the energy of an event in your business.

Learning from Your Sponsor and Upline

Your sponsor may not necessarily be the first person who showed you the business. As often happens, you may have heard about your business or product from one person and then actually decided to partner with someone else. You may have lost contact with the person who originally shared the company information, or just decided that another sponsor was a better fit for you. As long as that was your decision and not pressure from another sponsor, you should work with whom you feel comfortable and believe will get you to where you want to go.

 Essential

Your sponsor may not be the best mentor, but you can use her to help keep you accountable. Forward a list of targets you must meet every month, and then get together to review whether you have achieved them or not. Being held accountable by someone will help you reach your written targets.

Whomever you have chosen, your sponsor's role is to help you succeed in your business through proper training and mentoring. This doesn't necessarily mean your sponsor knows everything about what you need to know. It definitely doesn't mean your sponsor has to be perfect. But it is your sponsor's job to find the information that you need or connect with you with someone in your upline (the team members above your sponsor) who does.

A good sponsor will keep you informed of developments in the company and the product line. He will alert you to events you need to attend and where you should get tickets. More importantly, your sponsor is your partner in helping grow and develop your organization. This means he'll help contribute to your sponsoring efforts, perhaps by getting on a conference call or meeting with your prospect at Starbucks. Want a simple description of what your sponsor's role is? It's to give you and your organization a role model to follow. Your sponsor should set a standard and be the example of expectations within your group.

 **Question**

What do I do if my sponsor moves to another company or stops helping me?
You're an independent business owner. While it is your sponsor's responsibility to help you, circumstances may change and that help may not be there. Simply look to the person who sponsored your sponsor and see if you can work in partnership with her. Keep going upline until you find the person that is working the business and can help you.

A good sponsor will dig into your team and begin to work with potential leaders so that the whole group benefits. He should also be on any conference calls or webinars that he expects you to be on. Your sponsor must learn and know the company's system of growing an organization, and should be reasonably proficient at teaching it.

Just don't fall into the trap of thinking your sponsor will do everything for you. Remember, it's your business, and success in it is your responsibility. Your upline is your partner in making that happen, but they are not responsible for your success. Also, be sure you are always deserving of the sponsor's time by working the business.

During your very first days in the business, you and your sponsor should work out what the expectations are between the both of you and what you require from each other. Your sponsor wants you to succeed and will do anything within reason to help advance your growth. You should always be confident that your sponsor is able and willing to help you work toward your dreams. But no matter how excited your sponsor may be when you first join, there will be times when your sponsor may slip.

The Benefits of Personal and Professional Development

Personal development is the process of improving facets of your life, particularly related to the mindset and behaviors that can help you achieve your goals. This applies to both your business and personal life. It may mean you want to become a better communicator, less intense, or more assertive. Whatever you feel needs improvement, you can be certain there is a course or reading materials available that you can turn to for help.

Personal development is an ongoing, lengthy process, but that doesn't mean you will need to spend all your time focused on learning what to do. Just thirty minutes a day can do wonders for your mindset, attitude, and character. It is a pursuit that will grant you huge results in every other area of your life. There are hundreds of good books available to help you both work on your understanding of others and improve different parts of your life and relationships. Listen to a CD in the car, load up your MP3 player, or take the time to sit with a book and read a few pages—it all adds up! Look for material from authors such as Napoleon Hill, Dale Carnegie, W. Clement Stone, or Tony Robbins. Thousands of lectures and discussions on personal development are also available on podcasts that you can download for free.

It's not unusual for new reps to question the need for personal development. The fact is, no matter where you see yourself today and what you have achieved, it is the way you think and behave that has brought you to your current position in life.

It can often be difficult to get any further with the level of thinking you have today. Sure, you may get lucky and be in the right place at the right time, but you can't spend your life counting on luck. You need to be proactive and in charge, which means you need to work on developing the mindset and characteristics required to achieve what it is you want to achieve.

It won't be easy. It's not supposed to be. If having a charming personality, being an eloquent speaker, and displaying exceptional leadership skills was achievable by everyone, then people wouldn't have to aspire to get those traits. However, since the world looks for and values individuals that excel in the art of human interaction and achievement, you owe it to yourself to work on being the very best you can be, and to enjoy the many benefits of your personal-development journey.

Professional development, on the other hand, is improving your skills and expertise to achieve a desired business goal. Becoming a better recruiter, a more effective speaker, and knowing how to set up an event all come down to professional development. This is where you learn the nuts and bolts of what to do and how to do it. You'll often hear a rep say that she doesn't care for all the "mindset stuff;" she just wants to know what to do. This is the type of person who values the professional side of building a business over the personal development side. However, these two facets should never be separated. And if you are planning on building a thriving, well-trained organization, you will need to master both.

To build a business that lasts requires you to play many roles: leader, diplomat, confidant, teacher, and student. You will experience every conceivable emotion, from exhilaration to disappointment. Your network marketing business is an ultimate reflection of your life, with ups and downs, good times and bad.

But how could your business, dealing with products and services, reflect your life? Realize that you are not simply working with products or services and a business system. Your real product is people. People move product and create sales volume. People recruit others to the team and support them. People ship you the product, cut your commission check, and organize the next event. Everywhere you turn, everywhere you look, the very essence of network marketing is people working in partnership together. And people, being human, have emotions. They get frustrated. Some of them take a long time to grasp simple ideas. They quit. They join again. They will get you angry. People will surprise you and exceed your expectations.

Fact

There are many top income earners in the industry who never understood the compensation plan or intricate details of their product. They simply perfected the art of inviting and presenting, then used company material to educate their prospects and their team with more detailed information.

If you want to be able to work with the different personalities on your team, understand their character, and gain their trust, then you have no choice but to work on yourself first. Compassion, understanding, positivity, and optimism must be a part of you first before you can recognize and share those traits with others. When people start to look to you for leadership, support, and encouragement, you can't have an empty cupboard. The months and years you spend being ambitious and accumulating every positive attribute possible will make you a great partner and leader, and your recruits will be grateful to be on your team.

When you combine a positive mindset and attitude with the professional skills needed for success in this industry, not only are you destined to create an unbeatable team, but you have also developed yourself into an unbeatable human being.

CHAPTER 18

Becoming a Network Marketing Professional

Your business shouldn't be viewed as a hobby or a "little thing on the side." It's in your best interest to treat your business as if you had invested $100,000 into it. Just because you only put in a few hundred dollars to get started doesn't mean you can't develop an income equal to or above the most successful business owners you know.

Take Your Business Seriously

Be disciplined in how you plan your time and complete the required activities. Organize an area in your home, no matter how small or awkward, where you will be "in business." Your greatest advantage is that you can work anywhere as long as you have access to a phone and the Internet, but you still need somewhere to place your computer and keep product samples and prospecting tools. Being in business means you need to keep proper records of your income and expenses for tax time. Run your network marketing business in the proper, professional way and it will reward you for a lifetime.

Let your accountant know about your business, and ask for advice in what you need to provide when it comes to submitting your taxes. There will be many items you can use to offset your income, but your best bet is to work with your advisor to make sure you meet the guidelines set by the tax office. The rules and regulations change so often that it's best that you keep in contact with your advisor to make sure everything you do is above board.

 Essential

Your family and friends will respect your work time as long as you act as though you're working. Don't let them disturb you and they will soon come to understand that this is as much of a job as if you commuted to an office every day.

Every year the federal government and state governments pass numerous tax law changes. Many of these changes affect small-business owners because the tax system is frequently used to stimulate or hold back the economy. For this reason, most people who own small businesses rely on a bookkeeper, certified public accountant, or attorney to do their business taxes. If you have an accountant or other qualified person file your taxes, this person's business usually accepts at least some of the liability if something is done incorrectly. More important, however, is the fact that these people are paid to stay current with the laws and regulations.

On your part, do your best to keep track of everything that pertains to your income, expenses, and business activity. Most of this is easy to track as it is provided by your company. But you should still do everything possible to keep records that make it clear you are operating a business.

Every small-business owner—even those who are involved in network marketing part-time and make only a few extra dollars—must pay taxes that include the federal income tax, state income tax, self-employment tax, and state sales taxes. By working with a tax preparer, you will find many deductions and special tax rules that apply in each of these areas.

Alert

Don't make the mistake of forgetting to put away money to pay your taxes (and if network marketing is your sole occupation, you'll pay taxes quarterly). Your accountant will alert you as to what you owe once your tax forms are completed. Many self-employed business owners have been caught out with no savings put aside to pay this debt.

If you feel it is necessary and your income becomes quite significant, also talk to an insurance advisor regarding any coverage you may need for your business. If your family relies on the business for its livelihood, you can consider business interruption insurance. This insurance provides a portion of your typical earnings if the business can't operate because of an event such as a flood or tornado. However, be aware that most of these policies take effect only after a certain number of days. If you own a vehicle that is used primarily for business, there may be special policies that apply and would be advantageous to your portfolio.

Ethics and Integrity

The principles your team members live by come from the culture you create in your organization. You want to be very particular toward the kinds of habits and philosophies you start, build, and sustain. These habits will collectively form your team culture. This is why every team member, including yourself, must take ownership of this responsibility in order to support long-term, sustainable growth for everyone.

You can't build a large organization if there are team members who think it is okay to lie and cheat. You'll lose people at the drop of a hat if they feel the leaders have no morals or ethics. The foundation you build must be set on honesty, integrity, and trust. And remember: this is a business of follow the leader, so it has to start with you.

Of course, you can't control everybody's actions, but you can apply certain behaviors that help bring about a cultural shift in any organization. These include:

- **Punctuality.** Respect time. It's something you can't get back once it is spent. Be early at live events so the event can start on time. Also take into account that your team members will generally arrive around the same time you do. If you are consistently late, they will be too. If you are in charge of a business presentation, start and end it on time. If you say it starts at 7:30 P.M., don't start at 7:45 P.M. And do not go over the allotted time for a presentation (generally one hour). The worst thing you can do is have a presentation go on and on. Most of the recruiting will be done after the meeting, so be sure that you allow enough time for people to stick around, ask questions, and have the opportunity to join. If there is not enough time allowed for this part, you will find your prospect rushing out to get home.
- **Professionalism.** Be professional in your conduct, including the way you dress, the language you use, and the way you treat others.
- **Dignity.** Don't get dragged into gossip or speaking badly of others. From time to time, you may come across someone who does not treat you with the respect you deserve. That comes when you deal with large groups of people. Report it to your upline and then move on. You will often find those people do not stay long as your culture is not to their liking.
- **Gratitude.** Be grateful for the opportunity you have, your team, and all those who are supporting you. This will attract more prosperity and grateful people into your team.

- **Integrity.** Don't lie, exaggerate, or make things up in order to bring people into your business. They will find out the truth eventually. Don't steal other people's prospects. Do what you say will do.
- **Loyalty.** Be loyal to the company, the products, and your team. This will ensure that your people will be loyal to you.
- **Respect.** If you want respect from others, it's important that you respect others too. Ensure that respect is a core value in your team.
- **Supportiveness.** Be supportive to whoever needs it. This models the right behavior to all your team members and reminds them that they are not alone in building their business.
- **Personal responsibility.** Remember that nobody owes you success in this business. Your success is in your hands; it's your own business. Don't look to blame others; take ownership and responsibility and be mature about working through any difficulties that may arise.
- **Dress and appearance:** Dress professionally and respectably at all times. Keep in mind that professionals from other businesses will look and judge your business by the way you dress and appear. Keep away from shorts and T-shirts at business meetings. Be conscious of those in your organization that dress provocatively or sloppily. Dress like someone that you would want to follow.

While in a perfect world you would love it if everyone played by the rules and did what was right, you know that is just not going to happen. From time to time you're going to see people do the wrong thing. Don't let that throw you off. And don't always feel the need to play judge and render a verdict on their actions.

This industry has a fascinating way of dealing with those who believe they can shortcut the road to success, especially when they do it by hurting others. The best you can do is apply the principles you feel are correct and never be swayed off course by engaging in dishonest activity, no matter how enticing it may be in helping you reach your goals faster.

What People Look for in a Professional

A huge part of growing a successful team comes down to attracting the right individuals that will either join you as a rep or choose to become your customer. A good product and great company are just part of the equation. Your prospect is also looking to work with someone who runs the business as a professional. She wants to trust you to be able to coach her, provide the answers she needs, and help her reach the goals she has set.

She's not looking for someone who has a half-hearted interest in the business and is constantly unaware of new developments or standard information that applies to all reps. She wants someone that has the potential to become a real leader, that she knows takes the business seriously and has made the decision to build with her. This doesn't mean you need to be a brilliant public speaker, a witty and charming conversationalist, or know every minor detail of your compensation plan. It's more about being yourself, with your own distinctive character and personality, and applying yourself to learning everything you can about what it takes to succeed with your company.

 Fact

When a group of leaders surveyed new reps and asked why they decided on their particular company, the number one reason listed was the belief that their sponsor was professional enough to be able to offer the proper support.

Your prospective partner will be deciding from the first time she meets you whether you have the traits of a professional. Consider the way you are dressed and your appearance. Are you in generally good health and look like you take care of yourself? Is your car clean and tidy? Do you speak well, avoid vulgar language, and are aware of particular sensibilities with those you converse with? Are you punctual and respectful of the fact that most people are usually rushed for time and are going out of their way to meet you?

When it comes to your company and product, do you have a good overall grasp of your product line, compensation plan, and the company itself? Do you know when your next event is, and do you actually have a ticket for it yourself? Were you at the last convention, or did you miss it because the Knicks were playing that afternoon? Have you been promoted to the next level since you got started, or are you still getting ready to get ready after joining your company four years ago? Your prospect is considering all of these things and more, even if she does not tell you directly. She knows that a good sponsor, a strong and committed partner, will become a vital part of her business. If her sponsor is a professional who knows what she is doing and can teach it, then it goes a long way toward reaching success.

The smartest thing you can do now is work on becoming that professional. The information in this book is a great start, but the educational process is never ending. Constantly work on maximizing what you know and how well you do it, and the results will begin to show in the caliber of prospects that begin to say they want to partner with you.

The Power of Branding

What do your prospects see when they first view you online? How about when they meet you in person? What impression do they get regarding the opportunity you are aligned with and the people you keep company with?

The perception you create is the essence of what can be called your brand. It is the total package of the image and perception you have created, which reflects in how people view you. Branding does not only apply to business; it applies to people like you too. Everyone that meets you makes a rapid analysis and judgment regarding the way you appear and carry yourself, and that becomes part of your branding.

 Fact

In 2006, psychologists from Princeton University published an article named "First Impressions," which revealed that it takes just a tenth of a second to form an impression of a stranger from his or her face.

One of the best strategies you can use in your business from day one is to work on developing your personal brand. Take it as seriously as you take all other aspects of building your business, as many of your future team members are currently unknown to you and will only consider being part of your team based on your perceived brand and reputation.

Start by being trustworthy. This business is built by being open and honest with your team. You want them to know you can be trusted—not just with keeping secrets and telling the truth, but in doing what you say you will do when you say you're going to do it. Be consistent. Once you set a system in place for getting something done, stick to it. If you tell your people that there is a weekly webinar that they should be listening to every week, you have to be on it first. If you talk from the stage about recruiting new team members and you have not sponsored anyone in months, that is a flaw your team members will pick up on. Begin to look at every possible way you can show your commitment to your team and the company you represent. Are there weekly meetings you should be at? Are you in attendance at all the major events, particularly your company's convention? When there is a conference call, does your team know, barring an unforeseen circumstance, that you're always listening in on that call?

Reliability is also a huge plus in your personal branding. Your team members will gain confidence in knowing that you participate in all the business-building activities and that you are consistent in your commitment.

The Internet, particularly through social media, has given network marketers a massive boost in terms of creating their own online personal brand. From your profile picture to what you choose to share via words and images, you are being judged, and a perception about you, fairly or not, is being formed. It's important that what you share on the Internet displays the right image. Mistakes in this area can be costly. An offensive political rant, unsuitable comments regarding religion, or an inappropriate picture could have many people online choosing to distance themselves from working with you.

 Fact

Professionals will often look outside of their own industry for ideas to grow themselves and their business. Look for the gems in every business book and magazine article you read. If you find just one thing to help you, that's a success.

Choose instead to share posts of you helping other team members earn their first check or helping customers with your product. If you travel often while building your business, post pictures of where you are and the fun you are having there. If there are special promotions that your company has announced that prospects may be interested in—such as a great discount on a product or an enhancement to your range—be sure to let people know about it and make it easy to contact you to get the product.

There are other valuable reasons of why it helps to brand yourself in the right way:

- **People join you, not just your company.** When your prospect is evaluating your opportunity, he is not just looking at the company and its products. He is looking to see if you are the right person to be working with and trust his future to. This is made even more critical when dealing with prospects that have only recently met you.

- **People will follow you.** While ideally you would love to be a one-company networker, there are many reasons you may have to move from one enterprise to another. Your company could go out of business. The company may change the compensation plan or product line, and you no longer feel it is what you originally joined. You may simply find that the company is good for many others but not the right fit for you. There are many reasons that could be out of your control, and it may simply be down to personal choice. If the time comes to change companies, make sure people know and understand they will get the same exceptional treatment that is part of your personal brand.

- **Your company may change its policies.** Maybe you won't be able to sell its products online or keep your own website. Perhaps your strategy of promoting through Facebook is now not allowed due to changes in the agreement. Whatever the change, if all you have promoted is your company, your marketing is in trouble. If you have learned to create a personal brand, you can now start to focus more on you instead of the products or your business.

A common strategy to effectively brand yourself is to provide value to your followers through your past experience or skills you have developed either during your business building or prior. People want answers to their problems. Most networkers want help with their business building. If you can provide these solutions, you will add to your branding.

 Question

Are only full-time networkers considered professional?
No. Professionalism in this industry is based on the way you conduct yourself, not on your income or time commitment. You can be a professional from day one if you decide to adhere by the standards that the best professionals abide by.

Continue to attend company events and training in the areas of personal development and leadership. This will give you plenty of information to share with those who see you as a trusted leader. Share what you learn, and keep yourself open to interacting with your followers so you can ramp up your trust with them.

Creating your own brand is not an overnight process. It takes work and a lot of patience. But by staying consistent and working on providing value, people will learn to trust you and be open to your suggestions.

CHAPTER 19

Habits of Successful Network Marketers

Network marketing is a wonderful opportunity for most people, but it isn't right for everyone. If you prefer a fixed income and regular work hours, network marketing might not be a good fit for you. However, if you have the drive and desire to work for yourself, you can succeed in network marketing. You need just a few key personality traits to ensure your success.

Write and Review Goals

Every journey has an ultimate destination. And every destination is reached through a series of paths and points that the traveler has planned for prior to beginning the voyage. Success in business and life works very much the same way. Being clear about what you want to achieve and then mapping out a route to get there is not only good business practice, but it's a commonsense way to work toward most of your life's major goals.

Successful network marketers are aware of the power in setting goals, and they use this key principle to guide their business development and keep track of what they have achieved and where they may need to adjust their sails. No matter where you see yourself right now, whether you are in the business to earn a few hundred dollars a month or want to earn a full-time income, learning the skill and discipline of goal setting will give you enormous benefits when it comes to realizing success.

Goal setting works because it helps you clarify and zero in on what you really want to attain. By setting the goal, you also gain a great sense of what it is that you need to make it happen. There's no point in investing in tools that have no bearing on what you want to accomplish. By setting the goal, you also put into motion the thought process of what you will need in order to achieve it.

Goal setting also helps you keep the big picture in mind. You already know there will be plenty of distractions and things going wrong as you build your business. That's just the nature of the beast. You can easily get bogged down and beaten if you think that every roadblock can't be overcome. By having the ultimate goal at the top of your head at all times, you'll begin to see that, no matter what happens, achieving your goal is where it ends, and nothing should get in your way.

You may have a goal to sponsor twenty-four new people this year, at two a month. It's halfway through your second month, and you've yet to introduce a single new recruit. Do you stop now because you're already off the mark? Or are you determined enough to focus on your ultimate goal and realize that as long there is time and energy to get the job done you will make it happen?

Your network marketing goals may include a variety of targets including the number of people personally sponsored, a level of sales volume, or even the number of presentations you want to make on a monthly basis. Many companies may even set some of these goals for you, offering an incentive for their achievement.

No matter how the goals are set, they must reflect what you want to achieve both personally and financially. They should also be written down, with a deadline for their achievement and a stated reward for what you get when they are reached. Make sure these rewards are exciting enough to motivate and keep you going.

Writing them down is essential, as the process of writing, particularly by hand and not on your computer, smartphone, or tablet, will help your mind develop an imprint of the emotion and words used while you are scribbling down the goal. Then be sure to review them often, making needed adjustments when required and taking stock of where you currently are placed and what you need to do to reach your target.

Practice Listening and Communication Skills

Whether you are selling a product, selling your company to a prospective new team member, or helping a member of your downline make it through a difficult time, you need to know how to listen. When you think of a "typical" salesperson, however, you don't often equate good listening skills to that personality type. You know the type; these people have the answer to your problem before you even finish describing what it is.

Good listeners, on the other hand, gain business because they truly understand what someone is looking for. If someone comes to you and says she hates spring because there is so much gardening work to do, it's your job to find out if she just likes to complain, is looking for sympathy, likes to talk about her hobby, or has real concerns you can help her with (such as providing the hand lotion that keeps her hands from getting chapped when working outdoors).

 Fact

Most of your prospect's objections will be based on what you say first. If you are getting the same objection often, take a look at what you are saying in your invitation or presentation to be causing it. One word could make a big difference.

Good listening makes for good communication, and in this business, good communication skills are a major stepping stone to success. Good listening means you learn to ask questions that help the speaker feel you are interested in what she has to say. Why, when, who, what, and where are all good first words to use when replying to what someone just said. Listening to the answer doesn't mean you have to provide a solution or a similar story. You just need to let the speaker feel you are genuinely interested in her response and understand her point of view.

Stay clear of the common bad habit of changing subjects so you can now vent your own issues. Your prospects want you to guide them to solutions, not the other way around. If you think that by unloading all your personal and business issues onto them they will more likely feel that you are someone worth working with, you're going to be in for a lot of disappointment. No matter how mundane or monotonous the discussion becomes, as long as the subject matter is theirs, you should be the ideal listener.

Make sure you are attentive to the person who is speaking, because he will be totally aware if your attention may have drifted. If your Facebook update is more important than your prospect's next question, you are doing yourself a major disservice and you're wasting the prospect's time. Unless you are a doctor on emergency call, or you're expecting a call from one of your children, be disciplined enough to ignore your phone. If not, it's better to turn it off while you talk business with your prospect.

Also, be aware of your body language during your conversation. Folded arms, turning sideways, and eyes that shift to every possible distraction are clues that indicate your lack of interest. Slightly leaning forward, nodding at the appropriate times, and even smiling often can help the speaker feel you are sincere in discovering more about him and the way he feels.

Recognize and Encourage Team Members

Successful network marketers make recognizing achievement a mainstay of their team building. Your team members love to know that no matter how big or small their progress, acknowledgement will be made of their step forward. For many of your team members, any form of recognition will be unlike anything they may have experienced in their normal working life. Perhaps all they have received in the past is an invitation to the office Christmas party or a gift card after a particularly tough week.

 Essential

Whenever you hear a great story you can use with prospects or team members, write it down so you can reference it later. People love to hear stories, and they are great for teaching lessons on how to build the business and creating belief in your product.

In network marketing, you will find constant opportunities to let your reps know you appreciate their efforts. Spoken and written encouragement must become a natural part of your process. You'll often find there will be team members who will do more for a mention by the leaders in the upcoming newsletter than what they would do for extra commissions. The belief that you are a valued member of the team is powerful and confidence building, a feeling that you should be working to instill into every single person who joins your team.

Look to what your company and upline currently do when it comes to recognition of team members; then be sure to follow with that program, adding in personal rewards to further encourage members of your organization.

Stay Focused on the Main Task

It's easier than ever to be distracted while growing a business. You not only have daily life commitments and work obligations, but your new network marketing business comes with its own set of duties to fulfill. This takes a lot of discipline and determination. Effective time management and a lot of assertiveness when it comes to taking care of priorities is essential.

If you're not focused on the main goal—the critical object you want to achieve—it's easy to go off track. This is one area that leaders in your company probably learned to control early. Jere Thompson Jr., CEO of Ambit Energy, has this philosophy: "Let the main thing be the main thing." This mantra alone has been an essential key to what has helped them become an energy giant in network marketing.

 Essential

Good time management is a combination of knowing what to say yes or no to. The larger your organization becomes, the more demands will be made on your time, and many of them have nothing to do with you getting closer to your goals. The faster you can work out what is truly important, the better you will be able to manage your time.

You must learn to develop a laser focus when it comes to achieving the main task. If you know you should be at the next company convention, but you're a few hundred dollars short of an airline ticket, it's not time to worry and sulk about how you are going to get the money. It's time to focus only on the end result—what you have to do to get there.

If you need to reach $500 in personal sales volume by the end of the month, stressing over last month's low volume isn't going to help. Your only attention now should be on who would be interested in purchasing a product from you and how many you can potentially contact. Focusing on the main task doesn't mean that you'll avoid any problems in reaching your goal. It simply means that whatever comes up, whatever seems to take you away from the main goal, you are resolute and committed enough to work through to meet your objectives.

Be a "Rainmaker"

To be known as a rainmaker in your company is a worthy compliment. The title has been traditionally used to describe sales representatives or corporate executives who bring in business at any time, in any environment, no matter what the circumstances or difficulties. In network marketing, you will often hear these types of reps referred to as "heavy hitters," and they are accomplished in helping create growth, have an exceptional track record when it comes to creating sales volume, and are consistent in bringing new team members and retail customers into the business.

Rainmakers become so because they understand the activities that need to be taken care of that will help drive their team forward. They don't spend time constantly updating their photos on Instagram, watching training videos on YouTube, and complaining with other team members about why the new packaging is colored purple rather than green or why their rates aren't competitive. There's a time and place for some of these activities, but rainmaker reps spend a majority of their time working on what needs to be done to grow their income, such as:

- **Constantly add to your prospect list.** Don't miss an opportunity to get out and spend time at locations where prospects for your products may be present. What you do online with social media is only a small factor. Nothing beats meeting people face-to-face, then determining who makes a potential prospect.
- **Invite prospects to view your business or products.** There's only a small chance people will find out about your business if you don't actively invite them to take a closer look. Good, consistent inviting of prospects to consider your opportunity is essential.
- **Present your business or products.** Find out what communication method your prospect prefers, then use it. You

must find the time to either sit in person, use a live stream such as Skype, or send an online presentation. Whichever way works and is most convenient to both of you, use it to make sure your prospect gets all the information professionally.

- **Follow up effectively.** No matter how excited your prospect is about joining, you can almost be certain that the job of following up will be up to you. Implement a process of professional follow-up that allows your prospect to know you are excited in having her as part of the team.
- **Get your new team members started correctly.** The process doesn't end when you sign up a new rep; it's just beginning. The way you set a new recruit up, the expectations you set, and the training you implement go a long way in helping the new recruit attain success.
- **Attend events.** Being at events will help strengthen your belief and provide leverage when it comes to training and motivating your team members. It's easier to get people to events than working with them one by one to teach the exact same thing.

There are many additional facets to building a business, but rainmakers focus on what they need to do to create momentum and a higher income. If you work on the activities just mentioned and do them well, you'll turn into the producer that companies love to reward handsomely.

Have a Plan in Place and Take Daily Action

It would be rare—actually almost impossible—to find a professional network marketer who did not have a plan in place for daily, weekly, and monthly business-building activities. It is easy to work on things that don't produce solid results, or even help with business growth, if you don't implement proper planning and commitment to a plan.

Your plan should include the time you have allocated for personal development (ideally a minimum of thirty minutes a day), recruiting calls, checking in with team members and customers, plus your own professional and leadership development. Don't forget to block out time for when you will be at training events.

 Essential

Running a business is a constant juggling act. If you're not careful, you can spend your days working hard only to discover that you aren't getting anything important done. Or you can spend your days focused on some activities and let other important matters accumulate.

A written plan works best, as you can refer to it often to help remind you of what your priorities are at any given time. You don't want to be someone who is unsure of what lays ahead on any given day and is driven by unexpected commitments. You'll soon find that the days will come and go without any real sense of progress. This is also an area where habits such as procrastination and laziness can severely affect your business. You'll have to work on weeding these characteristics out as much as possible so they don't sow the seeds of inactivity and a lack of results. By working to a plan, you'll create a much stronger sense of direction and feel that you have greater control of your time and business life.

Attend Company Events

Your attendance at company or private team events doesn't necessarily mean you are the guest speaker, host, or even have to be up on stage. However, attending these events is mandatory for any leader. Your team should be encouraged to attend these events with you, and you can be certain they are watching you (whether you realize it or not) and taking note of how you present yourself at the event. If it's a smaller event, say a weekly business presentation, do your best to make sure you are there early to help with any issues with setting up. You should meet and greet people warmly as they arrive, and spend a little time finding out about them. During the event, aim to sit at the very front of the room, where the speaker will often focus and where the crowd assumes the higher-income earners are seated. Do your best to dress and carry yourself in a way that anyone entering the room rightly assumes you are a leader in the business.

Follow protocol by making sure your phone is turned to silent at all times during the event, and make sure you are taking notes in order to share with those who cannot be there. You must be in a position to share with your team highlights of every event and plan with them how you are moving forward with the information shared. Remember, sometimes you need the event, and other times the event needs you. Your support of events goes a long way in growing your own organization, and it helps support other teams too.

Acknowledge Other Leaders

As you progress within your company, it is inevitable that other leaders will begin to take notice of you and your achievements. They will see you on stage, hear your testimonial, or see your name on a company newsletter. Sensing your commitment to the company and your drive to succeed, you'll often find they have a different type of respect for you. It's not the common respect of acknowledging your decision to become part of an industry that recognizes entrepreneurship and self-determination, but a respect that is based on a mutual understanding of the changes, sacrifices, and effort it has taken to arrive at your present destination. Frankly, this is an understanding that only arrives with achievement. It's only when you go through what it takes to reach a certain level of income or a rank in your compensation plan that you can truly look to someone else and have a sense for what he or she has done to reach the same goal.

 Alert

If you're going to ask a leader in your business for advice, make sure you don't then challenge him on what he teaches. There's a good reason he is at his rank, and thinking you know more than him can seriously halt your income and group growth.

This is why it is vital you acknowledge other leaders on their efforts, and that you recognize what they have done in the business and respect their journey. Whether you are speaking on stage or privately with your team, make sure you are not belittling another team member's achievements or her story of what it took to make it happen. Learn to edify those that are in your upline and in other organizations in your company. Give them credit when it is warranted, and make sure that you are introducing them to new team members by weaving their accomplishments into the conversation.

It's important to remember that a company can only grow on the strength of its leadership. Your leaders, both in and out of your organization, will be happiest and most content when mutual respect and acknowledgment is practiced by all.

Share a Vision with Your Team

If you don't know where you are going, how will you know when you get there? This is the dilemma for leaders who work passionately on their vocation but are unable to clearly communicate a vision to their team of what they are working to achieve. Think of the late Steve Jobs, billionaire entrepreneur Richard Branson, or even your company's CEO. The one thing they all mastered is being able to share a powerful vision that inspires you to be a part of their mission.

 Alert

> If you have a "my way or the highway" mentality and you're losing people in your business, you may find that they think you are acting more like a dictator than a leader. Remember, this is a voluntary business; you can't force anybody to do it. The more they feel you have placed yourself as their boss, the faster they will start to lose interest in working with you.

Never underestimate the importance of a powerful vision. What is your vision? What can you do to inspire others? What is the mission you have that will make people stand up and take notice? Visualize it. Write it down. Look at how you will combine your network marketing business with the vision you have before you. Will you help create generations of people who are financially independent? Will you work toward building orphanages in Asia? Do you have a vision of taking your income and donating it to a worthy charity? Have a clear vision and deepen it into every fiber of your body, then go out and share it with the world.

Stay Positive and Enthusiastic about the Business

Network marketing takes a great deal of enthusiasm and persistence. You're going to hear a lot of objections, be let down by team members, and even be let down by yourself. It's easy to feel dejected and sorry for yourself, but you can't stay with that mindset if you want to move forward and succeed.

No matter what you are going through in your business, you must remember it is temporary, and it often takes just a little bit of motivation and a healthy dose of action to get out of your funk and back into feeling great. You can't control every aspect of your business, but you can control your mindset and attitude. That means staying positive, enthusiastic, and genuinely optimistic in the future you have ahead of you. By staying focused on the bigger picture and constantly evaluating where you are in terms of reaching your goals, you'll soon develop the habit of brushing off negative situations a lot more easily and taking on the day with a huge bout of enthusiasm.

 Alert

Make it a point to learn something about your customers every time you are with them. Don't just focus on the sale. Keep notes if you have to and refer to them before your next meeting. The more you know and understand their needs, the more likely you will retain them and they will refer other customers.

Your prospects, customers, and team members want to deal with someone who is excited about what they do and appears to not want to do anything else. This will help attract not only more team members, but it will lift the spirits of those you already associate with. Other people don't want to contact you to hear about your problems. They want to get on the phone or sit with you and leave feeling like they can take on the world!

By working on your own mindset, strengthening your belief in your company and product, and working over any negatives in your life, you can be the type of leader that people are inspired by and find a joy to work with.

CHAPTER 20

Advice from Professionals

O ne of the very best ways you can learn more about your business is to seek out mentors and leaders that have achieved what you want. Whether it's an income goal, a certain rank, or working on a certain skill or trait, network marketing has one thing in its favor . . . everyone around you is interested in your success. For your upline, your success helps grow their income and organization. For your downline, it helps inspire them to join you at the top and gives them the belief that you are a true leader in your company. From the moment you start your business, do what you can to find those people in your company you can learn from.

Meet the Experts

In this chapter, ten professional network marketers offer their thoughts on a variety of issues, ranging from recruiting new team members to developing better leadership skills to what they would do differently.

- Maria Ghaderi first got involved in network marketing at the age of eighteen. It took her six years of trial and error until she came across a company that launched her biggest success. Along the way she discovered a powerful mentor who helped shape her business strategy. Maria is based in Ontario, Canada.
- Goran Hemstrom is a former teacher, banker, and personal trainer. He builds his business full-time and has been a pro-

fessional network marketer for over two decades. Goran lives with his wife and two children in Melbourne, Australia.

- Wendy Man was first introduced to network marketing in 2007, living in Canada. Curious in finding out how the business actually worked, she applied all her prior experience in the import and export business to rapidly create success in her company.
- Nate Calima got involved in network marketing in college and has never worked a traditional job. He is based in Los Angeles, and uses his residual income to travel the world and expand his business.
- Jennifer Fisher, from Houston, got her first taste of the industry back in 2003. While the initial differences between network marketing and her traditional business created a culture shock, she quickly found success and today works her business full-time and is an advocate for women in network marketing.
- Raymond Tay is considered one of Asia's most successful networkers. He resides in Malaysia and has built massive organizations throughout Indonesia, Singapore, and his home country for over twenty years.
- Nattida Chong works her international business in partnership with her husband Chad out of their home in Los Angeles. Nattida graduated with business honors from California State University and dived straight into network marketing. She and her husband earned their first million in their twenties and now channel their significant earnings into an incredible lifestyle and to help fund their orphanage in Zimbabwe, Africa.
- Sarah Zolecki has over fifteen years of experience in the field, and has a contagious passion for helping people. She is widely known as a leader, building her international business with her husband Tony and their two children from their home in Minnesota.

- Jordan Adler resides in Las Vegas. He heard about network marketing in his twenties after reading a book he bought at a garage sale for twenty-five cents. He bounced from company to company for over ten years without making a penny. In 1992, he joined his twelfth company, and then went on to earn $20 million and become a top professional in the industry.
- Melynda Lilly started her network marketing career in Texas in order to stay home and earn extra money. Now with over twenty-six years in the profession, she has earned her financial freedom, not only for herself but for her entire family of three grown children and six grandchildren.

Recruiting New Team Members

You can't grow an organization without practicing the skills to recruit new team members. This is the lifeblood of your business. Recruiting is not always easy, as it takes belief in what you are promoting and the confidence to approach others regarding your opportunity. However, if you don't learn how to do it properly, your time in this business will be relatively short. By applying some basic skills, a good attitude, and basic common sense, you can begin to sponsor enough new reps to set the foundation for a solid organization.

Maria Ghaderi

In network marketing, you share an opportunity and enroll people to help change their lives. First you must believe that what you have will truly change someone's life. Belief in the industry and belief in your company is the key. The second is to come from a serving mindset. When recruiting new members you have to forget about how much money they will make you or the next promotion.

Raymond Tay

Constantly expand your list by exposing yourself to events anywhere there are people. As you become successful in terms of increasing income and personal development, recruiting new members becomes easier.

Nate Calima

This business may not be for everyone, but it's not up to you to prejudge the business for them. It's all about timing and proper follow-up. Life also gets better when you emotionally detach yourself from the answer.

Goran Hemstrom

Be clear about your objective. Understand that you are "sifting and sorting" to find those people that are ready, willing, and able. Your role is not to convince or sell people but to share your information. Ultimately you will become an extremely well-paid storyteller. Always use third-party tools to aid the presentation. Take yourself out of the equation and show your prospect that the tools will help them do exactly what you do. Be sure to then set a definite follow-up time and follow through.

Jennifer Fisher

Don't be afraid to offer your business to anyone, but learn how to get the conversation started. Don't chase after the undecided. People either want to do this or not. Only sponsor the ones who say yes and then take the time to teach them how to start and participate in the discussion of becoming a business partner.

Sarah Zolecki

Bringing new people into your business is all about connection. It's important that you look at things from their point of view—what's in it for them? You have to be able to convey to them the vision of what you are all going to do together. Make sure you know your vision.

Increasing Your Retail Sales

It's often assumed that retailing will be relatively easy, since most people understand the seller-buyer model. But you'll soon find out that retailing is also an activity that requires you to have a good mix of know-how, skill, and confidence.

Not everyone can see a need for your product or service. Not everybody will buy it at first glance. And no matter how much they initially show an interest, your customers may still find a need to throw in the odd objection or two to test you. Whether retailing a product or service, sales is mandatory in all compensation plans, so you must look at creating a group of customers who genuinely are interested in buying or using your product or service.

Maria Ghaderi
Be a product of the product. You can't share something you don't use or believe in. Using company tools such as catalogs, samples, gift certificates, CDs, or anything else that exposes the products to the marketplace can increase your sales. Home parties and trade shows also help with retail sales.

Wendy Man
Create more chances to meet people. Put some sort of promotional campaign together and combine products into an attractive package. Work on referrals with your customers and their friends and family members.

Goran Hemstrom
If they decide not to join the business, ask them to use the products. Then ask for referrals of people they know that might like to use the products. Simple, but effective.

Sarah Zolecki
It's all about customer service. Follow up with them after the sale. Ask questions. What do they like most about it? Ask them for feedback or reviews. Send them a handwritten thank-you card. Give them an incentive to give you referrals. It's all about the personal touch.

Melynda Lilly
Selling is just a matter of sharing. It's finding out what somebody needs and providing it. People hate to be sold but they love to buy. Believe in yourself, believe in the product, and believe in your company.

Developing Leadership Skills

There is a saying in the industry that everything rises and falls on leadership. While you will enter this business as a novice, you will soon discover the incredible benefits that are enjoyed by those who choose to become leaders.

Although network marketing leaders happen to be some of the most highly paid entrepreneurs in the world, it's not just about the income; it's also about the respect and recognition. It's about being a leader. Even if you feel you don't have the skills and attitude to become a leader in your company, you can rest assured that almost all the current leaders you see at one stage felt the same way. You won't just develop into a leader through osmosis. It takes time, effort, and experience. But the rewards are definitely worth it.

Raymond Tay
The fastest way to develop leadership skills is to quickly create a small group and lead by example by together doing prospecting, presenting, and enrolling. Lead by example.

Goran Hemstrom

Associate with leaders at events, through coaching, and on three-way calls where you simply listen to how they act and what they say. Read books about leadership and set time aside daily to listen to audio recordings by leaders from your company and within the industry.

Sarah Zolecki

Focus on one skill at a time, otherwise you can get overwhelmed or discouraged. For example, be punctual to events and meetings as a leader. Be impeccable with your word. Spend time with people that have mastered a specific skill set you need to work on.

Jordan Adler

What do leaders do? They lead. That means you do it first. In other words, you buy the products or service first. You set up the appointments first. You do the events first. The secret to leadership is you always do it first.

Jennifer Fisher

Leadership is not only about taking care of others, but yourself. It's about having done what those coming in will do and then guiding them through the steps to get where they want, listening to them, and encouraging them.

Working on Your Mindset

You'll soon discover that so much of what happens in your business revolves around your character and attitude. While a portion of your business building obviously requires the application of a few basic skills, the most important thing you can do is to work on the mindset needed to prepare yourself for success.

The road to prosperity is booby-trapped with disappointment, rejection, frustration, and a mountain of setbacks. It's difficult—almost impossible—to meet a leader in this business who did not endure some period where thoughts about quitting kept him or her awake at night. If you can manage to work through these frustrations, you will come out stronger on the other side with a greater sense of belief and increased self-confidence.

Nate Calima

Personal development and your philosophy is everything. The business is the simple part—it's the self-development that needs to be ingrained. You have to build an organization built on the right philosophies and culture.

Goran Henstrom

Pay attention to your goals. Write them down and ideally keep them visually in front of you (for instance, on a vision board). Be active. Those that are active and produce always have a great mindset. Read inspiring books and information that helps you to think bigger and better about yourself

Raymond Tay

Changing mindset is the hardest part because it's a long process. Have mentors around you who are more successful than you are, and continue listening to audio day in day out.

Sarah Zolecki

I work on my mindset at the start of every morning. I do a devotional, meditate, read, and study a chapter in a book and use audios or videos. Twenty to thirty minutes a day is crucial to setting your day up right.

Nattida Chong
The mindset is crucial in this business, and for life in general. It is vital for success. This business is 90 percent about your why and mind power, and only 10 percent hard work.

Mistakes to Avoid

From saying the wrong thing at an opportunity meeting to thinking you don't need to attend your company's convention, one thing you will soon come to learn in this business is that there are no new mistakes; there are only old mistakes being made by new people.

If you believe you're the first to incorrectly do anything, you are wrong. Somebody, somewhere, has made the mistake you did, and perhaps not just once. People make mistakes. That is a fact of life. What's important is that you learn not to do them again and discover ways to turn that mistake into a learning experience.

This means swallowing your pride and being humble. If you're going to move forward in this business, you need to be prepared to resist the urge in believing you are always right and simply give in to doing what can make you wealthy.

Maria Ghaderi
Not being coachable and trying to do things your way instead of the way it's been designed. Don't pay attention to negativity and get engaged with gossip and drama. Don't fail to follow up with your prospects or you may find the prospect has joined another team or a different company.

Wendy Man
Try not to act overexcited. Not everyone will share the same enthusiasm as you. Don't lose confidence so quickly after the first few nos.

Jennifer Fisher

Don't talk so much. In this business, the less you say, the more you make. Don't listen to the wrong people, doubting your success.

Melynda Lilly

Quit blaming other people. Don't start and stop your business. Don't take rejection personally. Stay away from people who distract you from your goal.

Jordan Adler

Avoid waiting until the time is right. The time is never perfect. Avoid "working with people;" instead, focus on getting people started. Avoid working the business based on how you feel. Work it based on your commitment, not emotion.

Nattida Chong

Don't quit before you even start.

Their Best Advice

There are no time machines (yet!) to drag us back into the past, but wouldn't it be great if you could take what you know today and apply it to the life you lived ten or fifteen years ago? You would have a great sense for how to handle various situations. You'd know exactly what skills you should develop before certain industries emerged and how your personal life could be improved, and you'd know those people to avoid and those you should pay closer attention to.

Network marketers experience many situations and learning encounters that lead to an understanding of what works and what doesn't. And many times, it is these things that they wish they could go back and apply to their first year or two in the business.

Maria Ghaderi

Stay more focused. Give yourself a long-term five- to seven-year plan and short-term (six-month) target. Join different social groups, communities who are interested in entrepreneurship, and make a list of two hundred and fifty people straight way.

Nate Calima

Believe bigger, sooner. Whether it's belief in the product, system, company, leadership, or even industry. Lack of belief will stop you from contacting your warm market and lack of belief will blast you out of the business once you have even the slightest objection.

Raymond Tay

Spend more time evaluating the company you are looking at before getting involved. Focus more on the success of your people than your own.

Wendy Man

Don't rely on your upline too much. It is your business. Don't get shaky every time you hear something negative about your company.

Nattida Chong

Believe bigger, faster. It will change the way you talk with people. The way you dress, your emotions, and so much more. Have a bigger belief. It will escalate your success.

Melynda Lilly

Get help. Find a mentor. Hire a coach. This is one of the best investments you can make in your business, Only work with people who deserved your time, not need your time. Set goals with new consultants from day 1.

Jordan Adler

Learn from your mistakes and failures. You can't have the front of the hand without having a back of the hand. Your story is not inspiring to anyone without the details of the struggles you have overcome, so embrace them. Those setbacks and experiences will make you who you are.

CHAPTER 21

Reaping the Rewards of Success

Although money is a wonderful goal, it is not the only barometer of a successful life. This industry can reward your efforts like no other endeavor, above and beyond the initial desire to create extra income. From the lifestyle benefits of free time and travel to the joy that comes with recognition and acknowledgment, the compensation on offer to anyone willing to build a solid business is drawing many to take part in the network marketing phenomenon.

What Network Marketing Can Do for You

According to a recent Harris Poll, people join direct-selling companies for a variety of reasons. Not all of them revolve around money, but when it is their motivation:

- Forty percent seek supplemental income.
- Twenty-three percent want to pay down debt.
- Twenty-five percent want to save for their future.

Without a doubt, it is the promise of greater income for a variety of purposes that opens most up to looking at a network marketing business. It's been shown over and over again that just an extra

$300–$500 a month can help keep many individuals from resorting to bankruptcy and their home being foreclosed on. While not everyone is looking to network marketing to work their way out of a dire situation, many can see the opportunity to build their business as an insurance against potentially hard times.

The beauty of this business is that you can practically sit down and make a list of what you want out of life, then build the business to meet the goals and dreams you have written down.

 **Question**

I don't really have a vision. I just want to get rich. Is that a problem?
Not necessarily, but chances are you do have some type of unrecognized vision. Ask yourself what you want to do after you are financially secure and it will become clear.

One of the greatest benefits parents see is the opportunity to bring together the family unit. What better way to teach your children the value of a dollar than to have them see exactly how you earn every penny? Anyone in network marketing can build a business that the family can contribute to, and even pass it down to successive generations. Many successful network marketers say they pursued this opportunity because they wanted a business in which the family could work together. They wanted a chance to get to know their children and guide them for more than just a few minutes a day, and to have a greater influence in their children's lives and decision-making.

Whatever your vision is, whether it's shaping your personal life or achieving material goals, you can take comfort in the fact you have joined a business that allows you the potential to fulfill your dreams.

The Value of Time Freedom

Besides creating financial freedom, this business is specifically designed to create personal time freedom, so you can do many of the things in life you really want to but don't have the time for right now. It's all about investing a little bit of your time now so you can enjoy a lot more freedom later. It's been said you can work hard for five years in network marketing and then take the rest of your life off.

With network marketing you can work when you want and where you want. Do you have a cabin you like to visit in the summer? That's just another opportunity to build a larger downline and create the free time to be there more often. Do you love to travel? This business can provide you with plenty of time and money to see the world. Looking for a little part-time money to supplement your full-time job? Weekends and evenings are great opportunities to work on your business.

Just be careful about being fooled by some sales pitches that can make it sound like the business is way too easy and only takes a few minutes a week to grow. Network marketing is still a responsibility, and you will need to invest time and money into it if you want to achieve your goals. However, you can decide how hard you will work, leaving you free to pursue your leisure activities when and how you want.

When you work for yourself, you can design a day that works perfectly for you. For example, if your downtime is 2–4 P.M., you can schedule that time to run personal errands or even have a massage. You can schedule work that requires enthusiasm, such as new business calls, for your uptimes. And you can schedule routine activities, such as filling out orders or watching the latest webinar replay, during the time of day when you feel most relaxed and don't have the energy to make recruiting or follow-up calls. Just remember that the return on your investment in network marketing is in direct proportion to what you put into it.

The Opportunity to Travel the World

Not many business opportunities give you the chance to create a national or an international business like network marketing. Your business doesn't need to stay situated in your hometown. If your company operates in other markets and other countries, there's the exciting option of taking overseas trips to help meet your team members and do a bit of sightseeing while you are there.

You can work to build your business in these overseas markets, or you can do what many reps do and use your income to finally take that long-awaited overseas trip to your dream destination. If you are traveling for your network marketing business, it becomes a very nice tax write off.

 Essential

A successful network marketing business means you don't have to ask the boss if you can take time off work or have limits on when you can go and come back. You are the boss!

With the free time you now have available, and your income being residual, you can be in Italy for two weeks and still have a business that is growing. You could be relaxing in Maui and find that another twenty new team members joined your team while you were having fun on the beach for a week.

Many team members make it a goal to attend as many overseas events that they can, not only to gain from the training, but to visit countries they may have never even thought of traveling to before. That could be a goal for you if your income allows it.

The pyramids in Egypt? The Eiffel Tower in France? A Buddhist retreat in Thailand? What is that one overseas destination that you would love to see and experience? Where are you dreaming of heading to once time and money are not an issue? Begin to think about it now. Write it down. Get pictures of these locations. Then work on making these incredible trips a reality.

Residual Income

Once you begin to truly understand the benefits of residual income you'll also catch on as to why so many business owners and private investors see the creation of a residual income stream as a must. The wealthy have all discovered the power of passive income.

Many people love the idea of having an income coming in whether they are working or not, but have no idea of how to make it happen. And they're often unaware of how network marketing is close to the perfect vehicle to create residual income.

If you have made the decision to join a company, you should be sitting down with your sponsor and working out what level of income you would like to create and what you will need to do to create it.

 Essential

Almost every compensation plan allows for the generation of residual income. As long as customers have a need for your product or service on a regular basis, you can create an income that continues to be paid to you over and over, often willable to your children and future generations.

Imagine living a life where you know that on a certain day every month your income was going to be paid to you whether you worked your business that month or not. If it sounds too good to be true, then perhaps you should go over your compensation plan again and look at how to make that dream entirely possible.

It's great to be paid well for your efforts every week with a salary. It's satisfying to know you have created a profit in your conventional business to divide among stakeholders. But perhaps the most rewarding type of income of all is residual. Do the work once, do it well, and get paid over and over again for years to come.

Create an Income for Retirement

There are many reasons people may choose to work past retirement age. One is that they genuinely enjoy what they do. Others love the social aspect and mental stimulation. And sadly, a growing majority are working into their golden years because they are financially incapable of retiring.

Many that are stuck in this predicament did not plan on being in this position. They imagined living out their retirement years traveling the world and spending time with family, perhaps taking time to relax at a lake house or on the beach. But due to circumstances out of their control or a lack of proper planning, they find themselves spending what should be the best part of their lives flipping burgers or working the graveyard shift at the local gas station.

Could network marketing have been their way out? Could this type of business be the perfect solution to a generation of senior citizens who are facing challenges they were never prepared for?

 Fact

While we often associate retirement with being sixty-five or older, the network marketing industry has allowed reps as young as in their twenties to retire permanently from the workforce. No longer needing to work is not based on age but on the fact that you have enough financial resources to never have to work again.

Wherever the answer lies, there is one thing you can control and that is the income you can have flowing in when it comes to your own retirement. You can be part of a business that allows you to set yourself up financially for life that can help you not only create financial security but true financial freedom. It is going to take work, but you can begin today to put in place an asset that will help you enter your retirement years secure in the knowledge that your income needs are totally taken care of.

Personal Development

Most reps enter this business focused on creating more money or on achieving some sort of material goal. Your neighbor may have spotted the new red Benz in your driveway that you earned as a car bonus and suddenly becomes fixated on getting one herself. A coworker joins you after realizing your yearly conventions were constantly being held in locations that he would love to visit himself. Every team member has his or her own personal reasons for joining. But the one goal that nobody even considers, but is almost the most talked about, is the personal development you will experience in being part of this industry.

The mental growth you will undergo, the boost in your self-confidence, and the development of your leadership skills will impact your life to the point you will not even believe you began where you are today. The change in some people has been so profound, so exhilarating to see, that many have proclaimed that network marketing is actually a leadership program disguised as a business.

That may sound scary to you. That is normal, as most people are afraid of change, particularly if it involves their own beliefs and character. Just understand that the change will be of your choosing, and will be gradual and nonthreatening. You will develop not just because you need to but because you want to.

Be open to the suggestions from your leaders when it comes to the resources you will need to foster this growth. Spend the time necessary, those crucial thirty minutes a day, to invest in your mindset. Before long, you will also be in the special group who understands that, above all else, it's who you become in building this business that is the most amazing reward of all.

Develop Into a Leader

It's not easy to think of yourself as a leader in your first few weeks in the business. You probably look at others who are known as leaders in your company and feel that you could never be like them.

They appear confident, full of knowledge about the company and the industry, and portray all the traits in their walk and talk that give the appearance they are real leaders. Would it surprise you to know that he was never like this just twelve months ago? Or that she was a nervous wreck who couldn't even recall the name of the company let alone parts of the compensation plan just six weeks ago?

He came into meetings and planted himself at the very back of the room, praying that nobody would notice he was there or ask him to share a testimonial. So what happened? The same gradual process that transforms anybody into a leader in this industry and in life. The very same process that will transform you if you allow it.

It's a combination of personal development, professional development, and leadership practices that will sink into every facet of your being. You'll begin to model yourself on other leaders and subconsciously apply the very behaviors that account for their success. You will mix with enough role models and influencers until the way you speak, the way you move, the way you interact with others has those around you convinced that you are a leader as equal to other leaders in the industry.

This is not an overnight process. It could take months, or even years. But eventually, as long as you immerse yourself in the activities required and stay in the environment that is network marketing, you will begin to see the effects that becoming a leader will have on your income, your family, and your future.

Help Others Achieve Success

This business works so well because we focus on helping others achieve success in order to create our own. You can't develop an income in network marketing until you have helped others with either your product or business.

Every compensation plan is structured so that your progress is dependent on how well you can support other reps in your organization. Many companies have even introduced matching bonuses—percentages paid to the sponsor that are only due when you help the rep actually earn an income—as part of their plans. Whether you sponsor a friend or a stranger, the goal remains the same: to help that person achieve the goals she has set and discussed with you. Remember, you don't use people or take advantage of them. You are there to help them, to guide them to what they seek to achieve.

There are people you know that desperately need a second income. Some require your products. All you have to do is be the one that asks how you can help and then offer a solution. They may have no interest of course, but they may also say yes and end up changing their whole life thanks to you. Also be aware of the help you can provide others who may so no to your business but you would still love to help in some way.

 Alert

> You can help others achieve success, but don't get trapped into doing everything for them. Remember, if you take away the struggle, you also deprive them of the joy of the victory.

You will likely have many things you would love to help others with. On your prospect list will be dozens of people whom you would love to see leave their frustrating job or be given the opportunity to travel more. This business works when you take your eyes off yourself and work on supporting the dreams of others.

The late, legendary sales trainer Zig Ziglar famously proclaimed, "You can have everything in life you want, if you will just help enough other people get what they want." This is a powerful principle that applies not only to life in general but especially toward creating success in network marketing.

A Positive Role Model in the Community

Today's society is crying out for positive, inspirational role models. While our youth take their cue for how to behave, what to wear, and what to eat from those they see in movies and music videos, we have seen an unfortunate decline in role models who are actively and personally involved in their daily lives.

Parents are so busy working to put food on the table and creating enough money to pay the bills that they are either too exhausted or lack the time to spend with their kids and provide the proper example their children are looking for. This desire for a role model continues on after youth, and many people continue to search for those they can emulate and follow even into adulthood.

Network marketing has an uncanny ability to produce members in our society that fulfill our needs of a role model—leaders who are financially secure, lead incredible lifestyles, spend quality time with their family and friends, and live with integrity, passion, and optimism. And these leaders are taught from day one that in order to succeed in this industry they must work to impart these qualities to others.

It is this very arrangement that causes leaders in this industry to become great role models, not only to those in their company but within their community as well. Having men and women that are financially stable, lead with an entrepreneurial spirit, and display exceptional personal qualities can only help strengthen our society and the world in general.

When you decide to become a leader in this industry, by default you have also elected to become a leader around those who spend their life around you. Family and friends will be inspired by your willingness to take on more responsibility. Other business owners, even outside of this industry, will feel a bond with you in knowing you are a believer in free enterprise and have the opportunity to set your own course.

Your example, and the way you react in many areas of your life, will be viewed and imitated by many others, including your children, friends, and business team members. What is the example that you want to set? Are you now living the life you want your children to model? And what can you do, beginning today, to start making the changes you want to see in not only your life but in the lives of those you influence?

Our society desperately needs great role models. Our families need them. Our religious organizations are in eager need of them. And businesses only thrive when they are present. You can make the decision, through the income, education, and experience you will gain from your network marketing business, to become the role model that people are desperately looking for.

CHAPTER 22

The Future of Network Marketing

A s many industries continue to slow down or disappear, and economic circumstances make it difficult for the average employee to find long-term job security, network marketing is a business model whose time has arrived. The DSA reports that almost 200 million new representatives worldwide have become involved in the industry since 2006. As education regarding the business improves, and success stories emerge from every corner of the globe, network marketing appears set to benefit our economy for many years to come.

A Glimpse Into Tomorrow

It's difficult to take a close look at the network marketing industry without being excited by its potential. Public acceptance is at an ever-increasing rate as professional training resources and educational opportunities regarding the industry continue to be developed. Entrepreneurs such as Donald Trump, Richard Branson, and Warren Buffett are not only advocates of the industry, but they have in some cases invested heavily in their own network marketing establishments.

Financial authors David Bach and Robert Kiyosaki have urged their readers to look at network marketing as a positive asset toward creating wealth and an exceptional training ground in relation to entrepreneurism and self-employment. An article published in *Forbes* magazine recently suggested that those who were concerned about financial security in their retirement would do well to look at network marketing as a solution to funding their later years.

These strong recommendations and powerful advocates, coupled with daily stories emerging from everyday people finding success in the industry, have developed the perfect springboard for the next stage in the industry's development.

Over the next ten to fifteen years you're going to see a greater surge of professionals, such as accountants, lawyers, and managers, look to this industry to diversify their incomes. This will in turn create greater interest with many who were once opposed to this industry and are now intrigued as to why their friends have chosen to become involved. In addition, women will emerge as powerful influencers and financial powerhouses, with a large part of their income derived from having created massive worldwide organizations.

The mainstream media will begin to feature many of the products you now see in network marketing. That has already begun, with primetime programs regularly sharing the benefits of products sold via network marketing.

 Fact

Looking younger, better health, and financial security are often listed as the three main desires of today's customers. All three main benefits can be realized through network marketing.

Parents who are looking to bring the family unit together and are tired of late nights in the office will join forces and build something from home that can give them financial security and time freedom. They want to be at home when their children leave in the morning and when they return from school. They want to spend time with them shooting hoops on a Sunday afternoon, without stressing over having to finish the accounting reports that are due at 7 A.M. on Monday morning.

Technology will make building your business both enjoyable and simpler. Applications that make it easier to share information and provide instant answers will be in abundance. State-of-the-art presentations about your opportunity will offer your prospects the full picture, with immediate options available to provide feedback and answers to their questions.

Network marketing companies will continue to be at the forefront of providing every outlet possible for anybody who chooses to partner with them to realize their dreams. Cutting edge production facilities and products that will create massive buzz in the marketplace will help reps feel confident and excited about their business.

While you can never truly know what technological advancement or new idea is about to make a splash in the market, we do know that network marketers have often been at the forefront of taking advantage of these innovations and turning them into productive tools that are used toward increasing growth and profit.

The Direct-to-Consumer Distribution Revolution

The Internet has not only given rise to a new information age, it has allowed the resurgence of a distribution model that for many years appeared stagnant. Delivery of products straight to the consumer was a commercial mainstay for many years as catalogs and flashy newspaper and magazine display ads promoted unique items that could be delivered straight to your door.

The retail giants did not wait long in providing a counterpunch. Greater variety and the opportunity to see and sample the goods before you made your purchase were hailed as the keys to a better shopping experience. For millions of consumers, these advantages seemed to outweigh the benefit of having deliveries made straight to their home at a small cost saving. Then the Internet arrived.

Goods that required no need to be handled first, or were well recognized in terms of quality and production, could now be ordered, with direct delivery, at costs that no retail store could reasonably compete with. Books, computers, shoes, and electronic equipment were being purchased with remarkable cost savings, and consumers took to the direct-to-consumer model once again in droves. Today online music, movies, and software have combined to create billions of dollars in sales where a physical product is no longer required. Speed of delivery, improved customer service departments, and consumer watchdogs working to ensure confidence in every transaction have turned direct-to-door purchasing into a convenient option.

Network marketing companies are fully engaged in this model: Distributors are no longer required to pick up their products from a warehouse, and "direct" distributors who would normally receive large quantities and be responsible for organizing their pick-up are no longer burdened with that task.

The Rise of Self-Employment

Millions of people, citing dissatisfaction within the workplace and lack of job security, are choosing to go out on their own and determine their own path to a secure income and happiness in their chosen livelihood. In the United Kingdom, an August 2014 report by the Office of National Statistics confirmed that the number of individuals who are choosing to work for themselves is at its highest level since records began to be kept in the 1970s.

Similar trends are being touted globally, despite new businesses often not meeting the expectations of those who have entered the self-employment arena.

These are just a few of the reasons why many are looking at network marketing and are impressed with the advantages over other potential businesses. While you can work privately out of your home, you also have a large organization behind you with people working toward a common goal while realizing their own personal objectives. The company you will work with provides basic business materials such as advertising, sales brochures, and online resources. People in your upline as well as at the home office are available to guide you through everything from setting up your business to teaching you basic selling, prospecting, and business management skills.

 Fact

Ninety percent of direct sellers and network marketers in North America work part-time from home, running their business in less than thirty hours a week. Most professional network marketers have learned to build their business working on average just ten to fifteen hours per week.

You also have more flexibility than most self-employed people. You don't have to work fixed hours because most of your customers are easy to reach in the evenings and on weekends. You can combine business with social visits. And eventually, when your downline becomes large enough, you can even decide to stop working altogether and enjoy living off the residual income that you have worked to create.

Network marketing is popular because it is uncomplicated and it gives you control over your life. What other type of business allows you to set your own hours and do exactly what you want to achieve your goals? Other small-business opportunities require you to put in specific hours or file special reports with other people in the business. In virtually every other type of opportunity that allows you to work at home, you are directly reporting to someone else who is in charge of making sure you get your work done.

Fact

Network marketing allows you to take control of your income. The harder and smarter you work, the more money you will make. If you just want a few extra dollars every month, network marketing can provide that. If you want to become a millionaire in ten years, network marketing can also help you make that happen.

With network marketing, you are in charge. You decide how hard you will work. You select exactly what work you will do. And you resolve how, when, and where you will get that work done. Nobody is looking over your shoulder forcing you to work instead of going fishing on a beautiful summer morning. No one is hassling you if you don't reach a quota or making you feel guilty for attending your son's school play instead of getting more sales made.

The Role of Women in Network Marketing

Women have not only featured prominently in network marketing's history and very foundation; they are now the driving force in creating a new generation of female entrepreneurs whose values are in line with the benefits available through this business.

A focus on supporting others, the opportunity to earn an income equal to their efforts, and the prospect of working from home around their family have provided women with a complete package when it comes to a venture well suited to their personalities and aspirations.

Women are not only having incredible success when it comes to building organizations; they are leading figures on the corporate side, with female CEOs becoming common within the industry.

It's estimated that at least 65 million women worldwide are involved in the direct-sales/network marketing industry today, and in the business world generally women are starting businesses at a rate of almost three to one over men in the United States. Many of these women are choosing network marketing as their business of choice, and the results are outstanding. Eight out of every ten women who earn over $100,000 per year are doing it through this business model.

Are all women getting involved in the industry to make that type of money? Absolutely not. Many are looking for a little extra income so they don't have to go out and get a second job. Others simply love the interaction and social benefits that come with nurturing a team. And many are genuinely passionate about the products they are marketing and want to share the benefits with others. Success in network marketing, whichever way you define your own success, is available to any woman who has a desire to create more out of her life and is willing to put time and effort into the pursuit of her dreams.

In August 2015, industry trainers Eric and Marina Worre, from Network Marketing Pro, hosted the Most Powerful Women in Network Marketing, a three-day convention that featured over twenty influential women in the industry. The thought of having an event like this just five years ago may never have even been considered; today it is seen as recognition of the increased role women are playing in the profession.

Societal Trends

Network marketing is incredibly flexible when it comes to adapting to environmental changes and society's expectations. When the compact tape cassette became popular in the early '70s, recorded music was the prime reason behind its surge. But savvy network marketers and shrewd company owners saw the opportunity to jump on this trend and began to distribute recorded information, which helped promote their company and provided information for both prospecting and motivation. This helped create a new generation of network marketers who would have previously never discovered the business unless they had attended a home or hotel meeting.

The industry continued to piggyback off trends that developed within both society and technology. The rise in use of the home computer, the move toward home-based businesses, and the growth of the self-employment sector helped create the perfect storm when it came to prospects saying yes to network marketing.

There is almost no innovation that has not been adopted by network marketers that has not helped create a greater awareness of the business and its products. From creating apps that help with recruiting and sharing information to running online prospecting presentations thousands of miles away, technology has helped networkers develop more efficient ways to spread the word and develop organizations around the globe.

The Home-Based Business Trend

The move toward working from home has been a major development that continues to support the growth of the industry. There are many benefits of working a home-based business, and many aspire to do so, yet the options regarding what to do from home can be confusing and difficult to navigate. While business owners are keen to develop something that offers true time flexibility, even around a family, the opportunities are limited. Network marketing meets this requirement, along with offering an abundance of bonuses that include the opportunity to travel, the ability to choose whom you work with, and the prospect of creating an income equal to or above any full-time income in the conventional workplace.

The Wellness Trend

The focus on health, wellness, and personal development has played an important part in the way we live for many years, and the movement only continues to expand. We not only want to look and feel better, but we're searching for alternative ways to create peace of mind and enjoyment in our lives. We now have a better understanding of the connection between stress and illness, the role good nutrition plays in our lives, and the need to relax every now and then and just smell the roses. While corporations have slowly adapted to this need in the workforce, the network marketing environment practically issues these lifestyle choices from day one.

If you are involved in a company that produces products in the wellness category, you'll find support from every avenue in terms of living a healthier and more active lifestyle. And if you are involved in any other form of product or service, you can be sure that living a better quality of life by freeing yourself of financial stress and creating more time freedom are themes you will hear about often and be encouraged to embody. The personal development factor also appeals to many as they get involved in network marketing, as they are inspired by the opportunity to both enhance their personal life and the lives of others.

The Social Media Trend

The rise of social media has created a culture that is more closely connected now than ever. We don't want to feel alienated or left out of a group; this has always been a part of our nature. But with social media, we can read what our friends are up to on Facebook or follow our favorite celebrities as they Tweet their thoughts. We feel closer to these people than ever before, with the opportunity to interact with public figures and those in the media now a common occurrence. But we're also finding comfort in discovering new friends and locating many from the past. This feeling of connection and community has shifted from the physical world to cyberspace, where a few passing comments online are enough to keep us feeling we are in the loop.

Where to from Here?

Uncertainty in the economy, favorable trends that support the growth of the industry, and an elevation in society's view of the network marketing business model has the industry primed to become a major player in this century and beyond. The only question that remains is how you will take advantage of it.

Network marketing offers a very real opportunity for realizing your dreams. It can give you both personal and financial freedom because of its unique attributes. It is a highly regarded, tried-and-true marketing and sales strategy that is going to become more important in the future. As consumers look for ways to simplify their lives and smaller companies look for ways to compete with large international conglomerates, network marketing will take on a greater role in the business world.

 Alert

Network marketing is gaining great inroads into conventional commerce, but you will still find many people who are unsure as to how it works or if it is legal. Make sure you are sharing professional resources when educating another person or business about this industry.

In addition, thanks to stronger government and industry-backed measures, consumers and prospective entrepreneurs are gaining greater confidence in network marketing as a valid and well-organized way to either purchase products or start a part-time, home-based business.

What else can be started with such a small investment, allow you unlimited income potential, afford the opportunity to travel, give you significant tax advantages, allow you to work with those you choose to work with, help increase quality time with your family, and be built part-time from home with nothing but a phone and the Internet? What other business would allow anybody, no matter your race, sex, age, education, or business experience, to build a worldwide enterprise that could continue to reward you with ongoing residual income for the rest of your life?

Perhaps the underlying factor in the success of the industry lies in this rare combination of factors. It welcomes its participants not based on where you are today but where you want to be. It opens its arms to anyone who is willing to receive its benefits into their lives. It is a business built on its members with two human qualities that reside in each and every one of us: hope and a dream.

No matter what that dream is for you, no matter how meek or magnificent you see your future, there is a home for you. There's a world of people who are ready to celebrate your success and encourage you on to greater heights.

As long as men and women continue to pursue a better way to live, where they can attain financial freedom and the lifestyle of their dreams, this industry will continue to prosper. Testimonials continue to pour in day after day, hour by hour, of team members who have achieved their dreams with this business. Now your amazing story is waiting to be told.

Welcome to the world of network marketing.

Additional Resources

Government and Industry Organizations, Consumer Protection

Better Business Bureau

www.bbb.org

This organization keeps a database of all the companies that consumers have complained about, no matter what the issue and no matter whether the complaint was legitimate or not. It also helps resolve complaints against companies.

Federal Trade Commission

www.ftc.gov

The FTC deals with high-level issues such as business privacy and curtailing monopolies. It watches network marketing organizations closely to ensure they are not operating as pyramid schemes.

World Federation of Direct Selling Organizations

www.wfdsa.org

The goal of this association is to support direct-selling organizations in the areas of governance, education, communication, consumer protection, and business ethics. It also lists network marketing companies around the world.

Associations of Network Marketing Professionals

Association of Network Marketing Professionals (ANMP)

www.anmp.com

The premier association uniting network marketing professionals worldwide—distributors, company owners and executives, as well as strategic partners of the network marketing community. The ANMP provides education and resources, and advocates for and celebrates not only the profession itself but also all those who are building careers and generating incomes within the network marketing community.

Direct Selling Association

www.dsa.org

The Direct Selling Association is the national trade association of the leading firms that manufacture and distribute goods and services sold directly to consumers. Approximately 200 companies are members of the association, including many well-known brand names.

Network Marketing News

Business for Home

www.businessforhome.org

An initiative of Ted Nuyten, CEO and chairman of the Business for Home Foundation, the website receives an estimated 4 million unique visitors from all over the world with the majority being network marketing professionals, with approximately 25 percent visiting the site looking for new or additional opportunities. Approximately three times a week a mailing is distributed to over 80,000 worldwide subscribers.

Inside Network Marketing

www.insidenm.com

Originally begun as a newsletter by Len Clements in 1990 called *MarketWave*, Inside Network Marketing focuses on historical trends and patterns that have resulted in success, and failure, by both distributors and companies.

MLM Help Desk

www.mlmhelpdesk.com

Troy Dooly provides breaking news and video analysis of events in the network marketing industry. He is a founding member and currently serves on the board of the Association of Network Marketing Professionals.

MLM Insider

www.mlminsider.com

MLM Insider was founded in 1991 by Corey Augenstein as both an information resource and watchdog publication on network marketing. Today the focus is on distributor training and education in understanding how the business works, particularly in relation to compensation plans.

MLM Watchdog

www.mlmwatchdog.com

Rod Cook has over forty years' experience in the industry and is an expert on analyzing compensation plans. His website compiles regular news and goes behind the scenes in relation to issues where there have been distributor complaints.

Success and Success from Home magazines

www.success.com

Success from Home magazine is a publication of *Success* magazine, which is designed specifically to serve the growing entrepreneur and provide personal and professional development. *Success from Home* is published once a month, twelve times a year, featuring a top network marketing company. The magazines can be purchased at most bookstores including Barnes & Noble and other retail outlets that sell magazines. A great read for inspiring and success stories of entrepreneurs in the network marketing industry.

Training and Education

Ambitious Women Success Club

www.ambitiouswomensuccess club.com

This club offers online personal-development training, as well as "coaching on demand." It is open to all network marketing women, regardless of company affiliation. Amy Applebaum, the Coaching Director, has been a lifestyle coach since 2002, helping women to build multimillion-dollar businesses. Taking her experience in business coaching, along with Esther Spina's MLM trainings and "hot topic" subjects, women are able to take their network marketing businesses to the next level.

Behind MLM

www.behindmlm.com

Network marketing information, news, and company reviews. The aim of Behind MLM is to be a useful resource to people curious about the industry and the companies that exist within it.

Direct Selling Mastermind Event

www.mastermindevent.com

Leadership event usually held in Florida in November, the Mastermind Event is a weekend of panel discussions and detailed training on what it takes to become a top producer in the industry. This is a generic event, and all distributors are welcome to attend.

Fortune Now

www.fortunenow.com

Tom "Big Al" Schreiter provides a considerable amount of training resources updated regularly that can help anyone with recruiting and building an organization. A free newsletter is also available, along with several complimentary audio downloads.

MLM.com

www.mlm.com

This site provides articles on network marketing strategies and a distributor forum that is regularly posted to. It looks at new companies and trends in the industry. It also lists products, suppliers, and a calendar of events for the industry.

MLM University

www.mlmu.com

Training resources and online classes by Hilton and Lisa Johnson, along with private coaching if required. A free e-newsletter is also available to subscribe to.

Network Marketing Pro

www.networkmarketingpro.com

In 2009, Eric Worre founded NetworkMarketingPro.com, which now has an audience in 137 countries around the world and a community of over 300,000 distributors. Since its inception, the site has provided over 1,000 training videos and hosted some of the most successful online and live events in the profession.

Network Marketing Times

www.networkmarketingtimes.com

Generic training tools, along with prosperity and success resources. Randy Gage's information is dedicated to helping those in the profession recruit faster, keep their representatives longer, and build long-term residual income.

Networking Times magazine

www.networkingtimes.com

Offers educational tools (books, audio, DVDs, online resources, live webinars) to help networking professionals and entrepreneurs acquire the practical skills and the right mindset to be successful in business and in life. *Networking Times* is a bimonthly educational journal focused on personal growth and professional development. The magazine is available on the newsstand in North America (in major bookstore chains) and online to subscribers worldwide.

PassionFire International

www.passionfire.com

Doug Firebaugh entered network marketing in 1985. His mission is to educate and instruct home business professionals. His website offers trainings on every subject related to network marketing.

RayHigdon.com

www.rayhigdon.com

Ray and Jessica Higdon provide ongoing mentoring and training through their blog and website. Regular audio and video training, and a special emphasis on building the business online, have made this one of the most popular training sites for marketers on the Internet.

Legal and Taxation Issues

Jeffrey Babener

www.mlmlegal.com

Mr. Babener is an attorney specializing in network marketing. His site offers updates on legal issues in the field, a list of conferences he conducts, and information on retaining his services. He also offers a newsletter, books, and audio resources on all facets of network marketing.

MLM Attorney (Kevin Thompson)

http://thompsonburton.com/ mlmattorney

Kevin Thompson is an MLM attorney and a founding member of Thompson Burton PLLC. Named as one of the top twenty-five most influential people in direct sales, he has extensive experience in helping entrepreneurs launch their businesses on secure legal footing. Thompson is considered a thought-leader in the direct-sales industry.

Tax Reduction Institute (Sandy Botkin)

www.taxreductioninstitute.com

The Tax Reduction Institute (TRI) is a tax education company located in Washington, D.C. TRI is involved in the creation and distribution of valuable tax information for independent contractors and small-business professionals, and has recently developed a software program specifically for those involved in direct selling.

Podcasts

Home Business Profits

Ray Higdon's podcast is designed for the home business entrepreneur that wants tips and tricks on online marketing, lead generation, traffic, attraction marketing, and also creating the right mindset for success.

MLM Nation

Simon Chan delivers this podcast three days a week, featuring an interview with a top network marketing earner who shares his or her journey and lessons learned. Each episode ends with the Million Dollar Question where you'll learn the first thing that the leader would do if he had to do it all over again and start his business from scratch.

Sales Refinery by Tammy Stanley

This podcast provides straightforward business-building advice that can have an immediate impact on your business and your bottom line. Tammy offers weekly free recordings, and her free download, "The 3 Simple Secrets to Attract More Business," is a must.

Street Smart Wealth Profit in Your PJs

Jackie Ulmer shares her series weekly, offering proven tips, tricks, and systems for creating wealth from home in a direct-sales business. She offers solid business and marketing techniques with plenty of blogging and social media concepts, and interviews other six- and even seven-figure income earners.

Unlimited Profits Training by Robert Hollis

Marketing and personal training for anyone ready to have a greater impact through their home-based business, network marketing, and personal development.

Books

Adler, Jordan. *Beach Money: Creating Your Dream Life Through Network Marketing*

Atkinson, Chris and Debbie. *It's Never too Late: Creating the Life of Your Dreams*

Brooke, Richard Bliss. *Mach II with Your Hair on Fire: The Art of Vision and Self-Motivation*

Carruthers, Brian. *Building an Empire: The Most Complete Blueprint to Building a Massive Network Marketing Business*

Covey, Stephen R. *The 7 Habits of Highly Effective People*

Crisp, Robert E. *Raising a Giant: Leadership in Network Marketing*

Dunn, Ken. *The Greatest Prospector in the World: A Historically Accurate Parable on Creating Success in Sales, Business, & Life*

Failla, Don. *The 45 Second Presentation That Will Change Your Life: Understanding Network Marketing*

Gage, Randy. *How to Build a Multi-Level Money Machine: The Science of Network Marketing*

Gage, Randy. *Making the First Circle Work*

Gage, Randy. *Risky Is the New Safe: The Rules Have Changed*

Hill, Napoleon. *Think and Grow Rich*

Kiyosaki, Robert T. *The Business of the 21st Century*

Klaver, Kim. *If My Product's So Great, How Come I Can't Sell It?*

Maxwell, John C. *How Successful People Think*

Robbins, Sarah. *Rock Your Network Marketing Business: How to Become a Network Marketing Rock Star*

Robinson, James W., and Charles W. King. *The New Professionals: The Rise of Network Marketing as the Next Major Profession*

Schreiter, Tom "Big Al." *Big Al's MLM Sponsoring Magic: How to Build a Network Marketing Team Quickly*

Schreiter, Tom "Big Al." *First Sentences for Network Marketing: How to Quickly Get Prospects on Your Side*

Schreiter, Tom "Big Al." *How to Build Network Marketing Leaders*

Schreiter, Tom "Big Al." *How to Get Instant Trust, Belief, Influence and Rapport! 13 Ways To Create Open Minds by Talking to the Subconscious Mind*

Schwartz, Dr. David J. *The Magic of Thinking Big*

Spina, Esther. *The Ambitious Woman: What It Takes and Why You Want to Be One*

Stanley, Tammy. *Carpe Phonum: How to Seize the Phone, Take Action and Call Your Prospects, Even When You Lack Courage*

Worre, Eric. *Go Pro: 7 Steps to Becoming a Network Marketing Professional*

Yarnell, Mark, and Rene Reid Yarnell. *Your First Year in Network Marketing*

Index